Celtic Wicca

Celtic Wicca

Ancient Wisdom for the 21st Century

Jane Raeburn

CITADEL PRESS
Kensington Publishing Corp.
www.kensingtonbooks.com

CITADEL PRESS books are published by

Kensington Publishing Corp.
850 Third Avenue
New York, NY 10022

All Kensington titles, imprints, and distributed lines are available at special quantity discounts for bulk purchases for sales promotions, premiums, fund-raising, educational, or institutional use. Special book excerpts or customized printings can also be created to fit specific needs. For details, write or phone the office of the Kensington special sales manager: Kensington Publishing Corp., 850 Third Avenue, New York, NY 10022, attn: Special Sales Department, phone 1-800-221-2647.

First printing October 2001

10 9 8 7 6 5 4 3 2 1
Printed in the United States of America

Library of Congress Control Number: 2001092058

ISBN 0-8065-2229-1

Contents

Preface

This book exists because I wanted to find it and couldn't. In it, I seek to provide a system incorporating both Celtic history and modern Wiccan vision while making clear which is which.

The Celtic path is deservedly popular: Besides supplying at least part of the ancestry of millions of Americans, the British Isles have provided the modern world with haunting music, poignant mythology, and a passionate creative spirit. It's hard to exist in American society, certainly, without being aware of manifestations of British and Irish culture, from long lists of Celtic-inspired music to rave reviews for Irish memoirs.

While it is valuable to study and learn as much as possible about ancient Celtic religion, it is difficult to structure a spiritual path from the historical record alone. Thus Celtic Wicca combines the most inspiring of ancient wisdom with the creative spirit and personal freedom of a new and modern faith.

For many years, authors have written about this path without clearly differentiating between modern inventions and ancient sources. Examples abound. In her valuable 1998 article "When Is a Celt Not a Celt?" Joanna Hautin-Mayer cites some of them: for instance, the writer who claims pumpkins (unknown in Ireland till 1588) were part of ancient Iron Age worship. In this book, I seek to offer a practical, respectful approach to the ancient material while encouraging you to use this knowledge creatively in your own life and worship. I also hope to communicate the joy, inspiration, and learning I've found in this religion.

It should be noted that there are books and groups that seek to re-create Celtic worship or culture without referring to Wicca. This is not such a book, though I have great respect for many who follow such paths. I believe Wicca provides structure and community that are important to most modern worshipers, as well as a wealth of creative ideas for spiritual learning and growth.

Though I've tried to treat historical facts with dignity, inevitably some mistakes may have crept in, and for them I claim full responsibility. Nonetheless, I also acknowledge the assistance of many who have helped make this book better, or who have inspired and taught me. They include Lakshmi, Darcie, and Stefen, who presided over my initiations; the members of Parth-Rathenroak, Avalon-9, and the Temple of Brigantia, from whom I have learned so much; and the members of the Maine Pagan Mailing List, who continually challenge and inspire me. Special thanks to Lilith McClelland, for starting all this, to Eric and Rita of Apple Valley Books for their knowledge and book-finding skills, and to Cynthia Jane Collins for extra support during the last few weeks of writing. Finally, to Cassius, my husband, best friend, and magical partner, I dedicate this book.

J.R.

Celtic Wicca

ONE

Overview of Celtic Religion

Celtic history is mysterious, ambiguous, and intriguing. The Celts themselves didn't keep written records of their lives, customs, or beliefs. We know many tantalizing bits of information—from archaeology, from the writings of the Roman Empire, and from early Christian writings that seem to retain some flavor of the pre-Christian world. These sources often fail to add up to a coherent whole. People of varying credentials have interpreted them in many different ways. And even the most eminent historians often disagree on important points. So please don't take this brief overview as the One Great Truth. Read the evidence for yourself. The answer to your question may well be "We're not quite sure."

For instance, who were the Celts? We first hear the term from a Greek writer, Polybius, and the Greek and Roman writers of the sixth through first centuries B.C.E.[1] mention variously Keltoi, Galatae,

---

[1] Recognizing the near-universal adoption of the Christian calendar, but wishing to respect all faiths, many modern scholars have adopted the terms C.E. (Common Era) and B.C.E. (Before the Common Era) with the same meanings as the Christian A.D. and B.C. I'm not a scholar, but I find this usage appropriate for writing about Wiccan and Pagan religions.

and Celtae. The people they refer to were the resident populations of Gaul (roughly where France is today) and the British Isles. Today's scholars use the word "Celtic" to refer to people who spoke (but did not write) variants of a common language and spread their culture across Europe in the Bronze and Iron Ages. While most people today use the word "Celtic" to refer only to the British Isles, many of the important Celtic archaeological sites are located in what are now France, Germany, and Spain.

Though the Celts didn't leave written records of their lives and beliefs, they were far from "primitive." They left behind evidence of a complex and effective social order, a distinctive style of decoration and artwork, and highly evolved beliefs. The values of creativity, passion, beauty, and honor, combined with the enduring mysteries of their existence, have endowed Celtic civilization with an irresistible appeal. American stores have whole sections devoted to "Celtic" music, and people of many nations spend time and money studying and visiting Celtic countries and their ancient monuments.

Unfortunately, even the facts we do know about the Celts have frequently been misinterpreted or just invented. For instance:

• *The Celts did not build Stonehenge.* It and many other stone circles, burial mounds, and *menhirs* (standing stones) were erected before the Celtic era, by Neolithic and Bronze Age people whose purpose and worship remain mysterious. There's no evidence that such sites were ever used ritually by Celtic priests.

• *There are no ancient Druid manuscripts.* Anywhere. Ever. Anybody who claims he or she has access to one is, at best, projecting a religious belief as historical reality. The priests of Celtic religion banned the writing of sacred knowledge, and instead transmitted their history, poetry, and faith through a memorized oral tradition that required many years' training.

• *The Romans did not stamp out the Celtic religion.* While some Druids were executed for their anti-Roman political and military activities, the conquering Romans left intact the religions of ordinary people, requiring only that local leaders pay token homage to the cult of the emperor's family. Indeed, there is considerable evidence that during the centuries of Roman occupation, practitioners of Celtic and Roman religion learned from one another, resulting in the blending of certain ideas and deities. Celtic religion was superseded by Christianity, not by the Roman gods.

• *Celtic women were neither ancient feminist heroines nor chattel.* New research is showing that the status of women in Celtic societies varied greatly from region to region. We know women were sold into slavery, but so were men. We know women were allowed to own property in their own right in many areas. Occasionally we hear of a Celtic woman ruling a tribe and leading it into war. In their worship, Celtic tribes honored both goddesses and gods, often (but not always) associating goddesses with land and sea, and gods with trees, animals, and the sky.

What we do know about the Celts comes from three main sources. One is the writings of Greeks and Romans who visited Celtic lands or encountered Celtic people as traders or slaves. These sources pose problems for the serious student, for such writers often wanted to portray the Celts as strange and barbaric people, the better to justify making war with them. In other cases, they wanted to depict the Celts as "noble savages," downplaying Celtic sophistication in an effort to contrast Celtic nobility with decadent Greek and Roman society. Even well-meaning writers ended up telling fantastic tales simply because they were strangers in language and culture to the people they tried to portray.

The second source is the artifacts, ranging from tiny bronze statues to burial sites to the remains of buildings and temples, which have survived the centuries well enough to impart some information about the people who left them. Here, too, we have difficulties, for such evidence must always be incomplete. For one thing, many of a culture's objects simply don't survive. Even when we find an object (assuming the site hasn't been raked over by clumsy archaeologists of another century, or raided to make building materials for thrifty farmers), there is often little information to tell us what it was for.

Was this bowl a sacred incense dish in an ancient temple, or a serving dish for turnips? Science can give us educated guesses, but few facts are solid.

Third, we have some written records from the beginning of the Christian era. These records (particularly the ones from Ireland, which never knew Roman rule) offer us some picture of Celtic society's values and laws. They come from a society that was largely Christian, and it is difficult to make assumptions about Celtic religion based on these sources.

So What DO We Know?

We know that the Celts existed, and that Celtic culture spread gradually into areas inhabited by Neolithic peoples. This expansion was not accomplished by a single conquest, but probably occurred through a combination of invasion, migration, and assimilation. We know that the Celts had distinct language, art, and customs, including ceremonies and rituals. We know that they had religious beliefs and practices, and we know enough about those beliefs and practices to make them the foundation of our own.

Celtic tribes formed strong spiritual bonds with the lands on which they lived. Towns, rivers, and mountains often had their own gods. Different tribes prayed to different gods for the same goals—successful crops, victory in battle, safety from natural disaster—or endowed the gods they shared with different attributes. Thus the god Lugh was associated with eagles in ancient Wales, but with ravens in what is now Lyons, France (a place once sacred to him under the name of Lugdunum).

Lugh was one of the most widely known and honored deities. Another whose worship is found across a broad range of Celtic lands is Brigid, whose name is variously written as Brid, the Catholic St. Bridget or St. Brigid, and Brigantia, from whom the tribe of Brigantes in northern England took their name. It's even possible, according to some sources, that her name was transmuted into Britannia, from which we get the names Britain and Brittany.

Lugh and Brigid offer a good introduction to two common arche-types of Celtic religion. He is a young god, associated with the sun, and while he is often credited with contributing to great victories, his chief attribute is brain rather than brawn. In Wales, later legends refer to him as Lleu Llaw Gyffes (Llew of the Skillful Hand); the Irish manuscript *Cath Mag Tuired* calls him Lug Lámhfhada ("Long-Hand"), for his throwing ability, but also credits him with many other skills. He is a god of the tribe, and his blessings make people's lives easier.

Brigid was equally popular, if not more so. She appears in legend as a goddess of the land. The Brigantes, the tribe who fought under her name, were known to the Romans as fierce warriors in defense of their territory, yet her attributes were primarily peaceful. In Ire-land, Brigid came to be associated with three areas of life: healing, smithcraft, and poetry. Like many other peoples, the Celts consid-ered the number three to be magical, and perceived many of their goddesses and gods as triples. In one legend, for example, Lugh was born as one of a set of triplets.

Lugh and Brigid were among the best-known Celtic deities, but they were by no means the only ones. Historians have found the names of hundreds of Celtic goddesses and gods. Many of their names are recorded only once, or only within a small area. Celtic worshipers believed each place, each river, each mountain had its own divine spirit, often a goddess. Other deities were associated with the sun, moon, sky, animals, plants, or skills.

In researching ancient religion, archaeology often leads us to focus not on how people worshiped during their lifetimes, but on their culture's beliefs surrounding death. This is in part because buri-als and cremations leave more evidence in the earth than, say, a fire ritual or an animal sacrifice, the remains of which are often indis-tinguishable from those of a feast.

Death is one of the great mysteries religion seeks to explain, and the burial practices of a culture can tell us much about what its people valued and believed. While many have claimed the Celts believed in reincarnation, the evidence is sketchy and subject to misinterpretation. Burying the dead with objects of daily life (clothes, shoes, weapons, pots) might be said to indicate a belief in some kind of afterlife, or may simply indicate offerings to the gods to honor the dead.

One religious concept reflected in Celtic art was the sacredness of the human head. The head was considered the most essential part of a person's body and was presumed to be the place where the soul resided. Sacred places were frequently decorated with representations of heads or niches with human skulls. A Roman writer, Diodorus Siculus, describes how Celtic warriors cut off the heads of those they killed in battle, then embalmed the heads of their chief enemies in cedar oil and preserved them. Thus the captor converted the power of the heads for his own magical defenses.

We also know that the Celts practiced both animal and human sacrifice. While these practices are considered repugnant today, they were common throughout the ancient world. Atrocities related by the Romans—for instance, imprisoning victims in a huge wicker-work figure of a man and setting the whole on fire—may have been propaganda intended to bolster Caesar in his war on the Celtic tribes of Gaul. But evidence strongly suggests that the sacrifice of a living person was at least an occasional event, perhaps to sanctify a holy structure or appease the gods during a time of crisis. Bones— sometimes animal, sometimes human, sometimes both—indicate the probability of animal and human sacrifice to win the gods' blessing on buildings or wells.

The most convincing discovery of this nature is the Lindow Man, a sacrificial victim of the Iron Age whose body was found preserved in a peat bog. His death was no mere accident or murder, for he was killed three ways: he was poleaxed, garroted, and had his throat cut.

Sacrifices were presided over by a priestly class called the Druids. The origin of this word is difficult to pinpoint, but may relate to a word for "oak," or another meaning "to know." Greek and Roman writers say these people (usually, but perhaps not always, men) had great power in Celtic society. They paid no taxes or tributes, and their duties also included healing, divination, judging, teaching the young, and keeping the calendar; in short, they were the educated class of their society. Druids may even have worshiped different gods from the ones worshipped by the common people.

A related group, bards, served as historians, poets, and satirists, and a few Celts impressed "cultured" Romans and Greeks with their achievements in these fields. While later Celts learned to write (Irish texts even designate a god, Ogma, as the inventor of writing), the Druidic culture forbade writing down the material of their religion. Instead, the ritual knowledge was passed from teacher to student via oral tradition and memorization.

Celtic tribes valued art, and objects of beauty and craftsmanship were offered to the gods in burials, in bodies of water, and at sacred sites. The Greeks and Romans described the Celtic fondness for boldness in personal adornment, but the treasures found in Celtic graves, bodies of water, and other ritual sites leave no doubt that craftsmanship was prized as well. Metal items were valuable and difficult to make, and the weapons, armor, and jewelry found in ritual well-shafts were true sacrifices, the giving up of something that represented a significant loss to the giver.

We don't know exactly what they hoped to obtain through these sacrifices. The gifts may have been meant as offerings to induce the gods to hear petitions, to protect a person or tribe during a time of trouble, or to promote survival and prosperity through fertile crops, successful business deals, and healthy families. They may also have been a form of status-seeking, a way of demonstrating wealth through conspicuously giving it away. In one fascinating article, the archaeologist Martin Bell speculates that some sites of ritual deposits may have been significant to the Celts because they were "wild" places in an increasingly agricultural landscape.

Relatively few pictures or statues of the Celtic gods survive, in part because of the Celtic leaning toward symbol rather than representa-tion in art. Indeed, the person just discovering Celtic religion is sometimes dismayed at the "crudeness" of Celtic depictions of their gods. The Celts had the skills to produce original and beautiful works of art. Why didn't they do this for their gods? Historian Miranda Green provides an explanation: The Celts, like some other ancient cultures, believed their gods transcended human form and mundane existence. Therefore, a depiction of such a god should transcend realism. Its very unreal appearance was a way of honoring the deity.

Another common way art helps us learn about Celtic religion is through the animals and trees accompanying a deity, indicating that deity's powers. The Celts' relationship with nature should not be romanticized (indeed, one scholar notes that Iron Age Celts cleared huge tracts of forest from the English Midlands, forever changing the region's ecosystem). Still, we can safely assume they were far more attuned to the cycles of nature than most modern inhabitants of first-world nations, with our central heating and supermarkets.

This relationship was sometimes ambiguous: Celtic tribes needed the natural world around them to be abundant with life, yet they also needed to destroy that life in order to survive. Thus we often see a local god portrayed as both protector of forest creatures and a divine hunter. In other cases, trees and animals have symbolic meaning. Birds often indicated the survival of the soul after death, while gods associated with boars claimed the animal's independence and ferocity.

Trees were especially sacred. Both archaeologists and the classical writers support the idea that Celts worshiped in sacred groves, often with a living tree or massive wooden post as the focus of veneration. In other cases, tribes dug pits or shafts, offered sacrifices of animals, food, weapons, or household objects to the earth, then "planted" wooden posts on top. In Gaul (now France), the thermal spring of the *Fontes Sequanae* was found to contain a rare relic: wooden religious statuary from Celtic times. The people who made these statues had a variety of trees to choose from, but chose oak heartwood for most of them. Oak trees were most commonly vested with religious power, and Pliny the Elder writes that the Druids conducted rituals to harvest mistletoe that grew on an oak; the mistletoe was then used to cure barrenness in women. Other trees, including ash, are mentioned as sacred, especially in the later Irish and Welsh stories, and various place names show variants of the Celtic words *bile* (sacred tree) or *nemeton* (sacred grove).

The coming of the Romans brought changes to the Celtic way of life and introduced new information to Celtic religions. Celtic tribes had a history of conflict with Rome. In 390 B.C.E., a massive army of Celts had swept into Italy and sacked Rome itself before accepting a large bribe to go away. The Romans devoted the next three centuries to building up their military, and by the middle of the first century B.C.E. the independent-minded Celtic tribes found themselves forced to form alliances with one another or with the Romans on one of two great sides.

The Romans conquered the Celts in stages. By the time Julius Caesar took command in Gaul (now France) in 58 B.C.E., previous generals had already defeated the Celts of what are now northern Italy, southernmost France, Spain, and Portugal. Over the next five years, Caesar largely (but not completely) subdued the Gallic tribes and began to look west to Britain. Between his first failed landing in 55–54 B.C.E. and the construction of the Antonine Wall in southern Scotland, which began about two hundred years later, most of Britain fell under Roman rule. Only Ireland and the north of Scotland remained independent.

What changes did Roman rule bring to the Celtic client-states and the religions of their people? Some champion the Celtic underdogs and condemn the Romans as repressive imperialists who callously destroyed the Druid priests. Others remark on the amazing religious tolerance Rome's conquered peoples enjoyed. The truth is somewhere in between. It's worth examining this period in further detail, because a great deal of what we know about Celtic religion comes from this time.

If you had been a rural dweller in Roman Britain, your religion might not have changed much from its pre-Roman roots. In towns, the Romans built temples and shrines on some Celtic sacred sites, and generally identified the local gods with their own. Thus a worshiper of the Celtic healing goddess Sulis could offer up her coin and prayer beside a Roman offering the same prayer in the same place to the same statue—which he called Minerva. It's important not to understate the changes the Romans wrought, particularly in the areas of temple-building and artistic style, but there are also distinct similarities between the two cultures' religions, such as the importance of the gods of a particular place. Over time, the Romans and Celts borrowed or combined deity names, attributes, and artistic techniques to achieve a certain degree of synthesis.

For instance, in what might be described as an attempt at a divine insurance policy, some people in Roman Britain and Gaul prayed to the Roman god Mercury in partnership with the Celtic prosperity goddess Rosmerta. Divine pairs are a hallmark of both Celtic and Roman religion, for the obvious symbolism of fertility (hence, increase of wealth and abundance) and as a way of combining religious traditions of the conquered and conquering peoples. Another technique was to combine two names that seemed to refer to the same deity—Sulis Minerva, for example, or Mars Cocidius.

If you had been a town leader or tribal king, you would have been required to pay homage to the cult of the divine emperor. When Roman rule was oppressive, as it was in the time of the war leader Boudicca, the emperor's temple was a vulnerable symbol; Boudicca's troops attacked the temple to Emperor Claudius at Colchester. Celts whose lives brought them into frequent contact with Rome were also exposed to new varieties of religion brought by colonists from around the empire, and mystery religions such as the cult of Bacchus may have achieved a following.

If you had been a Druid, you might have been killed or forced to flee your home during the conquest, for while the Romans tended not to interfere with local religions, they did object to a priesthood that used its political and spiritual power to organize military opposition. Druidry survived the time of battle, and was largely tolerated thereafter, but Celtic priests never again wielded serious political or military influence. Tacitus, writing toward the end of the first century C.E., refers to Druids hurling curses at the invading Romans on the island of Anglesey. He notes that the Roman soldiers stopped for a moment to gape at the "unfamiliar sight," which some scholars interpret as a sign that Druids in England had disappeared or at least gone underground. Some later classical writers also mention

Druids as philosophers or, intriguingly, as women who could foretell the future.

In the centuries after the conquest, Roman soldiers and leaders settled down in Britain, often intermarrying with the locals. In the centuries that followed, a recognizable type of religious art and architecture known as "Romano-Celtic" developed. A Celtic tribe might have worshiped outdoors in a *nemeton* (sacred grove); a Roman citizen might have worshiped in a stone temple with huge columned porticoes providing shade and a place to meet friends or do business. The Romano-Celtic period provided a simple two-story temple building surrounded by a single row of columns, often just large enough for one or two people to make offerings in a place sheltered from the weather.

In Ireland, which was never ruled by Romans, the Celtic religious material eventually became part of the native tradition of story-telling. Centuries after Christianity became the dominant faith of the island nation, early medieval priests and monks recorded the legends and stories of this land. Written down in the early ninth century C.E., the Old Irish story of the life of St. Brigit (perhaps the clearest example of the Christian absorption of a Celtic deity) includes a Druid, who understands Latin and warns the young saint's uncle of her Christian future. This may mark the beginning of centuries of stories about Druids, whose compelling mystery has perhaps now lasted longer than the Druids themselves.

The Druids died out. Of that there can be no doubt. By the time the Romans lost their hold on the British lands (around 400 C.E.), the Celtic religion was fading, too. Christianity had found favor with citizens of the Roman Empire, and was spreading, with a faith both puritanical and peaceful. By the sixth century, written evidence suggests Pagan religion no longer posed any serious threat to this dominant force.

Why did Christianity appeal to the Celtic people? Some of the reasons were the same throughout the Roman Empire. Women were often the first in a family or town to convert, lured by an emphasis on the stable family and the prohibition of adultery for both sexes.

Early Christianity also encouraged those men and women who preferred to stay celibate. Traders across the Roman Empire exposed
Celtic tribes to a greater world, which may have loosened their alle-
giance to the gods of their lands. Christian groups in many areas
began as burial societies, building community by guaranteeing each
member proper rites for the transition to the next world. And Christianity encouraged community and fellow feeling in a society that
was becoming increasingly stratified by wealth, language, and status.

Celtic faiths that revolved around a sacred king were left rather
flat when that king became a Christian. Folk customs did survive,
often changing and losing their original meanings with the suc-
ceeding years, but the actual worship of the Celtic gods fell away.
One of the chief criticisms that can be leveled at the early Chris-
tians is that they destroyed much of the art and architecture of the
old religions, smashing statues and temples, and burying or burning
the objects of Celtic veneration. In a few areas, Celtic holy places
became the sites of churches. In parts of England, Anglo-Saxon
invaders imposed their own religion, derived from Germanic roots,
before converting to Christianity, adding another layer to the already
confusing historical record.

So passes Celtic religion from the records of history—if not from
the hearts of subsequent generations. Irish and Welsh chroniclers,
most of them monks, wrote down the myths of their lands. Despite
a Christian veneer and centuries of reworking, these stories are all
we have of Celtic mythology, and we will refer to them in the chapters that follow.

By the Renaissance, "antiquarians"—generally, educated men with
free time and an interest in history—had begun to dig up and
chronicle the sacred sites and artifacts of times long past. While it
has taken many years to correct some of the mistakes they planted
in the popular imagination, their interest laid the foundation for the
scholarship of today. As historians' total knowledge increases and
science provides better tools for understanding what we find, there
are exciting new discoveries to be made about these ancient people
whose spirit still calls to us. We will never truly know everything

there is to know about the Celts and their beliefs, and this mystery will always be part of the appeal of Celtic religion.

As students of this history, we must learn to live with ambiguity. We can know some of *what* the Celts did, but we can only guess at *why*. The best we can do is to craft a worship that draws a strict line between what is based in history and what is imagined in the present. This requires being honest with ourselves about what we know to have happened and what we think *ought* to have happened. It requires recognizing that some appealing ideas are not history but myth, spiritual beliefs rather than documented facts. It means keeping our minds open to the possibility that some of our information is wrong or misguided. The spiritual path outlined in these pages is one that attempts to hew faithfully to this line while honoring the vital spirit of the Celtic world.

Mental Exercise

Tapping into the Celtic spirit requires separating your mind a bit from your modern life, with its distractions and responsibilities. To achieve this, you need to learn to quiet your mind and develop its powers of concentration. Virtually all religious faiths practice some form of contemplation. But whether you call it prayer, meditation, or visualization, you'll find it comes easier with practice. This next section offers a couple of beginning exercises for someone who is just starting, but is also useful as a refresher for someone more experienced.

Because this introduction is intended for a Celtic path, I've tried to avoid Eastern concepts such as concentrating on *chakras* (power centers in the body) or meditating on a *mantra* (word or phrase), but by all means use these if they work for you.

The Druids, who were said to spend twenty years preparing for their priesthood, are not known to have practiced this or any particular form of meditation. The vast quantity of facts they were required to memorize, however, indicates that some form of mental discipline was necessary. Regardless of any historical background, meditation is a valuable tool for anyone seeking to develop a spiritual mind in the average modern life. Creating sacred space within your own mind makes room for the gods to enter.

Don't expect divine revelations right away. You'll probably find you need to spend some time just working on clearing your mind of the mundane and learning to concentrate in stillness.

CReating Meditation Space

Comfort and privacy are essential before you begin. This may mean setting aside a corner for meditation and arranging with family or housemates for a regular time during which you can remain undisturbed. Do this in the place where you are most comfortable. For most people, home is best, but others may be more relaxed outside or in a nondenominational chapel.

Most Westerners are not comfortable sitting cross-legged on floors. Unless you really like sitting this way, try a chair with arms instead. Make sure your back and neck are supported, and your clothing is comfortable. Meditating while lying down is possible, but one runs the risk of turning the meditation into a nap. If you are lucky enough to be able to hear the sounds of nature, listen to those; otherwise, you may wish to put on some peaceful, ambient music. Keep a notebook and pen nearby to record your experiences.

EXERCISE 1: CANDLE GAZING

This is a common starting point; the writer Starhawk recommends a version of this exercise in her popular Wiccan book *The Spiral Dance*. The point of this exercise is simply to help you find your own "still point." You start by using an external object as a focus point. A plain white candle will do, or whatever you have handy. If a candle is inappropriate—if, say, you recently survived a frightening house fire, or if open flames are not allowed in your living space—try substituting an image of one of the Celtic deities, or a piece of symbolic jewelry suspended over a black cloth.

Set the candle or other object of focus in front of you, making sure you can look at it for an extended period without straining your neck. Many people find it meaningful to remove glasses, contact lenses, or watches when doing meditations or rituals. Light the candle and look at the flame. You don't need to stare, just relax your body, taking deep, slow breaths, and look at the flame. Try to release all the other thoughts running through your head. Don't work too hard at this; it may take several sessions before you can focus even for a short while.

Thoughts will inevitably spring into your head. Accept them. Occasionally the gods reveal truths during this time; at other times, your subconscious may come up with solutions to current problems. But once you've looked at the thoughts, gently set them aside to analyze later, and turn your attention back to the flame.

Finally (and it make take a few sessions to get here) you will reach a point where the candle is the only thing in your consciousness, where your mind is completely still. Remember this feeling; it is a starting point for religious experience. The next day, try to hold the feeling a little longer.

After ten or fifteen minutes, stop and return the next day. It can be tough to fit a daily meditation into most busy lives, but those who do find it relaxing and renewing. In addition, repetition of this exercise (at least four or five times a week for the first two weeks) is important to getting your mind used to finding the still point. Once you've established this mental path, it will be much quicker and easier to follow; soon, you'll be able to get there without the candle.

EXERCISE 2: WATER GAZING

Here you will use the meditation time to find the answer to a question. This is one of the simplest forms of divination. It uses water, which is associated with many Celtic deities and myths. You'll need a wide ceramic or metal bowl about half full of clear water.

Think of a question. If you can't think of one, try something like

"What is the next step in my spiritual learning?" With your eyes closed, concentrate on the question for a couple of minutes. Without letting the question go, take your concentration away from it and open your eyes.

Gaze into the bowl the way you did the candle. Comprehend it with your eyes as you quiet your mind. When you have reached the still point, begin to listen to the thoughts that do come up in your mind. Again, don't stop to analyze the thoughts—just take note of what they are.

When you are ready to stop, turn your gaze elsewhere. It may be helpful at this point to write down the thoughts that came up during this meditation, or to speak them aloud to another person.

The thoughts at this point are coming through your own consciousness, so they may reflect whatever is floating through your psyche. The answer may be clear, or there may be nothing of any value. If you get nothing, don't blame yourself—just try again. A written record or tape recording of the question and the responses, with the date, may be enlightening in the future.

Once you've gotten used to using water as a meditation focus, try this exercise at a lake, stream, or at the seashore.

Exercise 3: Guided Meditation

In this exercise, you'll find your still point, then proceed down a pathway that's been established by someone else. This is a common use of the meditative state of mind. Guided meditations, also known as pathworking, visualization, or guided trance, are a staple of group rituals, as they assist in establishing a similar mental state in all participants. There are many versions of this "Tree Meditation," and it is commonly used as a relaxation exercise at large group rituals. I use it here because of the common theme of trees in Celtic art.

The most effective way to experience this mental state is to establish your own still point, then have someone else read the meditation slowly, allowing time between phrases so you can experience the inner journey. If you are working alone, you may want to read this over several times to establish the sequence before you begin, or make a tape recording, so that you need not interrupt your journey to check the text.

Before you start, take a few minutes to clear your mind and relax. Breathe deeply and slowly.

Imagine that your body is the trunk of a tree, standing tall in a forest. Feel how solid and strong you are. Feel your roots reaching deep into the earth beneath your feet, radiating below you to partake of the earth's nourishment. On each in-breath, feel the energy of the earth begin to rise slowly up through your roots, gently flowing upward into the tree. This is the strength of the earth, and is always there whenever we call upon it.

Feel the energy rise out along the limbs of the tree, down the branches. At the tip of each twig, it forms a drop of dew. On an out-breath, visualize the drops of dew falling gently back to the earth, creating a circle and a circuit.

Take some time to experience this cycle. On each in-breath, draw in the energy of the earth, and know that it is available to help you accomplish your goals. On each out-breath, feel the falling drops of dew taking away your stress, your mundane problems, your own limitations.

When you are ready, open your eyes.

If you have a special affinity for or interest in trees, this visualization may be clear enough that you can discern what species of tree you "saw." Consult a book of Celtic tree lore if you believe the type of tree had a personal or divinatory meaning.

TWO

Wicca

Wicca is a new religion, invented by people who wanted it to be an old one. While hearkening back to pre-Christian goddesses and gods and (in many cases) incorporating historical words and practices, most of the elements in any Wiccan ritual are more recent in origin. This may come as a disappointment to some who cherish the notion of an unbroken line of knowledge passed from ancient Pagans, but it also affords modern Wiccans a great freedom and responsibility: the power to create living rituals ourselves.

Where did Wicca come from? Like all religions, Wicca was not handed down directly from on high, but was crafted by real people who developed its concepts and wrote down its earliest texts. In this case, however, we know the names and histories of the founder, Gerald Gardner, and several significant early contributors. Beginning in 1939, Gardner and the first Wiccans—perhaps the best known is Doreen Valiente—drew on a variety of sources, including Freemasonry and other aspects of the Western occult tradition, for their ritual material. Another source was the writings of Margaret Murray, an early anthropologist whose history of the "witch cult" enjoyed wide popularity despite her failure to back up many of her points with evidence.

Following the lead of the Order of the Golden Dawn and other nineteenth-century occultists, the early Wiccans admitted women and men to equal practice and power. Their rituals and theology declared that nature and sexuality are gifts of the gods, to be honored rather than repressed and exploited.

Like the founders of many lodges and fraternal groups, they sought to invest their creation with legitimacy by crafting an "ancient" origin for it. As Aidan Kelly points out in *Crafting the Art of Magic* (one of the earliest works to explore the modern origins of the religion), obscuring the newness of Wicca also obscured the innovation and creativity that went into it.

Unlike many of the religions started in the twentieth century, Wicca is thriving and growing decades after it began. This spiritual path has proven strong enough to outlast most of its founders and early adherents, and flexible enough to be adapted by hundreds of thousands of different people, in ways its founders never dreamed of. Wiccans have their own theologies, their own ethics, their own sacred texts and their own priesthoods. Wicca is a "real" religion, and many institutions, ranging from colleges to the U.S. military, recognize the right to practice it.

Wiccans sometimes call themselves "Witches," and refer to their practice as "the Craft." Wicca is part of a movement called "Paganism," "Neopaganism," or "Earth religion," which generally seeks to honor pre-Christian deities and views nature as intrinsically sacred. In this book, we'll use Wiccan ritual structure to worship the goddesses and gods of the Celtic era.

By honoring the Celtic deities and culture within the structure of Wicca, we tap into a living, growing spiritual path, a framework in which groups can form and grow and newcomers can learn from experienced practitioners. Conservative estimates indicate that there are between one hundred thousand and five hundred thousand Wiccans and Pagans in the United States, with significant populations in Canada and the United Kingdom; with those numbers, a practitioner who is familiar with Wiccan ritual can often find fellow believers within a reasonable distance.

A few myths to dispel, for those who are new to Wicca: Wiccans do not worship Satan, believing him to be a Christian figure who lies outside our religion. Wiccans do not try to recruit others into our religion; indeed, we regard proselytizing as impolite, though we're happy to answer questions from those with a sincere interest. In addition, Wiccans are prohibited from causing harm to others or manipulating others' actions and thoughts (we'll talk more about this in the Ethics chapter).

The vast majority of adult Wiccans respect parents' legal right to govern their children's religious upbringing, and will not accept teenagers as students or coven members without parental permission. Parents who are concerned about their kids' explorations should get involved, learn about the religion, and seek out responsible practitioners, rather than ban all mention of Wicca and take the risk that their children will follow an unscrupulous or ignorant leader.

Some things Wiccans do believe in:

• *The "immanence" (direct presence) of the divine in nature.* In Wicca, nature is not the creation of a god—it *is* God, or rather a variety of goddesses and gods. As a result, many Wiccans work for environmental causes, learn about the natural environment of the place they live, and try to live in earth-friendly ways. At the very least, being Wiccan means a heightened appreciation for the beauty and power of nature.

• *The equality of male and female, and the worship of both goddesses and gods.* Because of this belief in equality, Wiccans' spiritual paths are not limited by gender, only by their own interests and abilities. However, some Wiccans worship only goddesses, feeling that Western society is so patriarchal that they must take the opposite approach to achieve balance.

• *Magic, sometimes referred to as "energy,"* a spiritual force that Wiccans believe emanates from nature. Within some limits, this force can be shaped to the will of the practitioner.

• *Spells, which are akin to intensified prayers*, often using a physical object as a symbol to reinforce one's intent, and calling upon one's own personal power to focus on a goal.

• *The interconnectedness of all things, particularly "correspondences" among systems of experiencing the world.* For instance, a day of the week or compass direction might be associated with a specific color, deity, metal, herb, magical purpose, tool, and planet, and might be associated with rituals or spells aimed at a specific set of results.

• *The sanctity of our own bodies, including our sexuality.* From the earliest Wiccan rituals, sexuality has been recognized as a sacred force, which can be directed like other forms of energy. Although Gardner himself disdained homosexuality, this attitude has long since been discarded. Wiccans are generally accepting of homosexuals and others whose preferences and identities are outside the mainstream. Ethical Wiccans know that this sanctity only intensifies the importance of behaving with integrity in one's sexual choices. In no case does it mean the right to harm or take advantage of others.

• *Reincarnation or the afterlife.* Most Wiccans refer to a "Summerland" or peaceful, pleasant place where the soul goes after death, only to be later reborn.

• *An emotional and spiritual connection to history.* This yearning was felt by the earliest Wiccans, which is why they "archaicized" their ritual books—wrote them in "old-fashioned" language—in an attempt to create a past for their new religion. The inspirational force of history has unfortunately led some Wiccans to believe inaccurate interpretations of the facts, or to ignore evidence that does not fit their beliefs or wishes. Nonetheless, many Wiccans are genuinely fascinated by history and interested in discovering the real truth of ancient cultures, and you'll often find their homes packed with history books.

If you feel drawn to the Celtic deities, Wicca offers many ways to experience these divine energies directly. To start, we'll explore some ideas for making your spiritual life a part of your home. I'll also offer two techniques for casting magic circles, the Wiccan's way of transforming any space into sacred space.

Your Own Altar

Because Wiccans can rely on their own energy to establish a direct connection with the gods, we usually set up altars in our homes rather than relying on a central one at a place of worship. Indeed, some Wiccan homes have altars in every room. A permanent altar serves as a visual reminder of your spirituality as you go about your daily life, and provides a convenient focus to help you meditate or pray. It's also a way to express in the physical realm the things that mean the most to you in mind and spirit.

You do need a space that is yours. For most people, it's possible to set aside a bureau top or small end table, preferably facing east or north. If that won't work—let's say you live with small children or destructive pets, or just live someplace without a lot of privacy—try setting aside a special place to store ritual implements. I put together my first altar while sharing a cramped apartment, and stored my altar cloth, candleholders, books, and Tarot cards in a wooden chest that had formerly served as my childhood toy box. Others have used a drawer of a desk or bureau.

If you can't set aside permanent space, or you plan to perform rituals in more than one place (perhaps outside in nature when the weather permits), try using a briefcase or picnic basket as a portable altar.

What belongs on your altar? Anything that reminds you of the deities of your worship, or that helps to enhance your meditation and visualization. There's no "right" set of implements for your altar, though there are some traditional tools and arrangements. Common altar objects include:

- Altar cloth
- Statues of deities
- Magical tools (see below)
- Objects from nature (leaves, flowers, stones, shells, plants, feathers)
- Candles and incense

- Pictures of deities or places in nature
- Any object appropriate to your ritual purpose

To start, choose an altar cloth (perhaps a silk scarf or decorative tea towel), add a candle (make sure the candleholder is wide enough to keep wax from dripping on the cloth), and choose one item that has spiritual significance to you. As you learn more, you can add more items, or change them around, but this first altar will serve as a place to focus your spiritual energies within your physical world.

While many people go to great lengths to decorate their altars, you needn't spend lots of money to make your space sacred. Many altar items can be handcrafted, which will infuse them with more of your personal energy. An altar cloth can be a remnant from the fabric store; pictures and statues can be your own work.

Your altar will most likely become the place where you perform your meditations. As your "higher self"—that part of you which carries your aspirations and makes the most direct connection to the divine—learns to associate this place and these objects with your meditative state of mind, you'll find that "still point" easier to achieve whenever you're at your altar.

I also find it helpful to light my altar candle to help me concentrate when I'm reading or writing. If you're stuck on a creative or intellectual project, try working on it near your altar with the candle lit. Since you've already learned to focus your mind in the presence of the flame, you'll find it easier to slip into a productive pattern of thought.

Magical Tools

The ancient Celts made images of their deities, and we have a Roman writer's account of the Druids using golden sickles to cut sacred mistletoe. There's also evidence that some Celts made spears or knives out of bone, and sacrificed them in ritual shafts and wells when they couldn't afford to give up their real weapons.

Beyond these tantalizing bits of evidence, we honestly don't know if an average Celt would have had specific objects used for religious purposes. To an archaeologist, a ritual knife or cauldron looks a lot like the same item used for more practical purposes. If it is buried in the ground or cast into a pool of water, it is hard to tell whether its owner was offering it to the gods, throwing it away, or trying to hide it from enemies.

The Wiccan tools are adapted from those used in medieval ceremonial magic, though the name "athame" for a Wiccan's ceremonial knife, is Gardner's own invention (possibly inspired by a science-fiction story!). Wiccans customarily do not use any of their ritual tools for non-spiritual purposes. The following set of tools has been common for several decades:

Wand. This is used when invoking deities or spirits, as well as directing personal spiritual energy. It can be merely a straight stick, but can also include decorations reflecting the owner's own spirit. The wand in Celtic Wicca is also a way of tapping into the energy of the tree.

Athame (ritual knife). Never used for cutting anything in the physical world, this knife should be small, with a handle that fits comfortably held in both hands. The blade is usually double-edged. It is used primarily for "casting circle" to create sacred space, and occasionally for rituals to cut oneself off from unwanted influences. Some pronounce the word "ah-THAIM," others "ah-THAH-mee" or "AH-tha-may." All are correct, since it's a made-up word; I prefer the last one, because it's what I was taught.

Chalice. Usually filled with juice or wine (less often, water or milk) which is used to toast the goddesses and gods. Many groups also pass the chalice as a way of sharing spiritual energy and community. This can be a wineglass, but many prefer something opaque, such as silver or ceramic, as a symbol of mystery.

Pentacle. In Wicca, the five-pointed star refers to various five-point systems of understanding the world. The most common ascribes the four lower points to the four elements of ancient Greek magic (air, fire, water, and earth) with the topmost signifying "spirit."

Wiccan altars often have a metal, stone, or wood disk with a pentacle engraved or painted on. This is used as a base for tools, and oaths are sworn with a hand on the pentacle.

You need not rush out and buy all of these tools. Indeed, you may decide not to use all of them. As with your altar items, you may prefer to make some of your tools, or to put personal energy into decorating or painting the ones you buy or find. Many Wiccan and New Age stores have attractive tools which may appeal to you. If they don't, it is perfectly acceptable to use something you already own, or something you pick up at a yard sale. The only important factor is your own personal feeling for the object. Before spending a lot of time or money on any tool, make sure it will fit in your hands, on your altar, and in the place where it is to be stored. Above all, make sure you like it.

Wiccan groups (often called covens) will sometimes pool their money to invest in a set of group ritual tools. Depending on the coven's resources and size, the wand, chalice, and athame may be replaced by a wooden staff, a cauldron, and a sword.

What to Wear

Traditionally, Wiccans are said to perform their rites in the nude, but in practice this is not an easy thing to do. Even if you can achieve privacy, you may frequently find yourself too cold, vulnerable to mosquitoes or stray drips of hot candle wax, or simply unable to shake the feeling that someone is watching. I recommend that you worship in whatever clothing is appropriate to your situation and enhances your concentration. If you find it meaningful to practice in the nude, you may still wish to have a robe or other ritual clothing for attending group rituals.

You will probably find it valuable to choose a robe or other garment that you wear only for ritual. Like your altar, your ritual garb can help you cast aside the worries of the day and enter a more spiritual frame of mind. If you're not ready to choose a complete ritual outfit, you might pick one garment or one piece of jewelry and set it aside to wear when doing spiritual work. For private workings, the only real criterion is that your attire be comfortable and easy to move in, without trailing bits of cloth that could pose a hazard when working with candles.

The standard Wiccan robe is long, black, and hooded, tied around the waist with a cord. Some groups require such a robe, others just say "wear black," and still others permit a great deal of personal choice. I attended a Spring Equinox ritual where participants were asked to wear spring colors; one gentleman expressed his feeling for the season by wearing a New York Yankees uniform.

Outline of a Wiccan Ritual

This introduction is meant as a rough guideline on what you might expect if you attend a public Wiccan rite.

Most ritual organizers will not allow you to "just watch," even if it's your first one. Why? Because the presence of an observer can throw off the concentration of the people participating in the ritual, and because you yourself won't experience the full energy of the ritual if you are outside the circle. A responsible ritual leader won't make you do more than follow along with the group, but will ask that you participate.

This outline represents a typical Wiccan ritual. Some rituals omit one or more of these steps, or add others, and you should feel free to experiment in designing your own ceremonies.

Preparation. The altar and tools are set up, candles and incense are lit, music plays, and the elements of the ritual meal are set out. Participants put on their ritual garments and go over what will happen in the circle and what will be expected of them.

Grounding and centering. Participants meditate, either as a group or privately, to calm and concentrate their minds.

Casting the circle. A priest or priestess, often using an athame, walks the boundary of the ritual space to sanctify it.

Calling the quarters. Someone goes to each cardinal direction (north, east, south, and west) in turn and summons the spirits (sometimes called "Watchtowers") of that direction to protect and guard the circle. This section often includes a call to the spirits of the classical elements (earth, air, fire, and water).

Invocation. Participants, usually led by a priest or priestess, pray to one or more goddesses or gods (often a goddess and god who together form a "divine couple") to be present at the rite and bless the ritual's goals.

Energy raising. For a work of magic, participants energize the circle through chanting, singing, or dancing.

Magical workings. This can be as simple as a meditation, or as complex as initiating a student. Some group rituals allow time for each participant to seek divine help with a personal issue. All participants should be informed of the goal of the magic before the ritual begins, and given a chance to back out if they are not in agreement with it.

Sharing of a ritual meal. This phase is often referred to as "cakes and wine," though you'll find all kinds of menu variations (bread and beer, cookies and juice, strawberries and mead). This shouldn't be a vast quantity of food or drink, just a ceremonial amount to forge a physical bond among the participants and the deities. If something is served that you prefer to avoid, just lift the cup to your mouth respectfully, or take a piece of the food without eating it. Leftovers are often poured or scattered outside after the ritual as an offering to nature spirits.

Ending the connection with the deities. It is considered improper to tell a god or goddess to leave, so participants usually restrict themselves to offering thanks and farewells.

Bidding farewell to the spirits of the four quarters.

Taking up the circle.

If necessary, a brief *meditation* to help participants ground the energy of the ritual and resume mundane life.

Often, a potluck supper, dessert, or snack follows the ritual, to allow time for socializing and grounding.

The Sacred Circle

While the idea of ritual celebrants gathering in a circle is nearly universal, the concept of a "magic circle" as a place where spiritual energy is gathered and directed dates back to Renaissance magical books, translated in 1888 by S. L. MacGregor Mathers as *The Greater Key of Solomon*. They became the foundation of most ceremonial-magic groups of that era. Gardner drew upon these groups' rituals in crafting early Wiccan rites, and thus the circle has passed into the ritual format of Wicca.

The rationale for it goes like this: Wiccans don't usually have a building set aside for their worship, instead performing their rituals outdoors or in their regular living space. So instead of putting up a church or temple, we use magic to create a sacred space for each ritual.

The ancient Celts didn't do this—at least, there's no evidence to indicate that they did. They did have sacred places, usually groves of trees, where they performed sacrifices and ceremonies. The Celts also built temples, some of them very small, where they went to pray and leave votive offerings, and offered sacrifices at sacred rivers, pools, and bogs. Such places were probably considered holy by their very nature, leaving no need for the worshiper to delineate sacred space.

So why do it? The explanation has to do with the nature of magical energy. Wiccans believe that magical energy is everywhere (rather like electricity), but becomes powerful when directed toward a goal. In casting a circle, you set a boundary within which energy can be "raised" and concentrated, rather like a battery. By casting a circle, we protect ourselves from harm or distraction, while focusing energy on the goal of the ritual.

On a more personal level, casting a circle helps to set the mood for a ritual. As you cast a sacred circle, you are saying with your actions, "Here, in this space, I intend to be my most spiritual self, leaving aside for a time the worries of mundane life." With repetition of these actions, your subconscious comes to associate them with a focused, receptive frame of mind.

You need not have a complex goal in mind for your sacred space; the circle is yours to cast any time you wish to do so. Almost any time you invoke a goddess or god, you will probably wish do so from within a cast circle, both to honor the deity and to bar unwanted entities. Many people also cast circles as protection for their spells and divination, but you may do so even for something as simple as a meditation. Repeating this set of actions helps you practice this element of ritual, and offers inner protection to you while your mind journeys.

According to folk tradition in Britain and many other countries, going around something in a clockwise direction (sometimes called "deosil") is considered lucky, associated with increase and abundance. Circling counterclockwise ("widdershins") carries the opposite associations. Wiccans have adapted this tradition so that circle casting goes clockwise, while taking up the circle at the end of the ritual goes counterclockwise. In groups, it is often considered impolite to turn or move counterclockwise during the rite, though this is sometimes unavoidable when many people are moving about a cramped space.

Preparing the Circle

Before you begin, prepare as if for a meditation, arranging for a peaceful and private atmosphere. Mark the boundaries of your circle using cord or chalk, or place stones or candles to indicate its limits. Wiccans customarily place candles at the four compass directions, with the altar in the north (sometimes in the east or at the center). If your altar doesn't face north or east, don't worry about it for now. The important thing is for you to build up magical energy in the space that's already your own.

Outdoors, you'll find that sacred space almost seems to create itself, particularly when you can find a spot that is both beautiful and private.

Some tips for indoor circle casting: When you are ready to start, turn off as much artificial light as you can, and proceed by the light of candles or oil lamps. If you like, add music and use incense or oil to lightly scent the area. Turn off the ringer on the phone, and make sure your candles and incense are moderate enough to keep the smoke detector silent.

While you're preparing, take note of the sounds, the smells, the temperature in your ritual area, and do whatever you can to minimize distractions. Attend to your bodily needs, adjust anything that is uncomfortable about your clothing, and make sure any items you will need are within reach. Wiccans and other magical practitioners regard the circle as a sacred boundary. Once the circle is cast, they regard it as a breach of etiquette to cross the line for anything short of an emergency until it is taken down. Experiment on your own. You will most likely find that crossing the boundary of the circle renders it less powerful.

Decide what you will use to cast the circle, and place the appropriate tool on or near your altar. If you have an athame, use that. If not, try a wand. You may even use your own hands, folded together with the index fingers outstretched, as a focus for your magical energy. Once you've gotten used to working with a magical tool, you can use almost anything to channel your intent. Not long ago, when I was asked to get a "tool" for circle casting, I came back with a screwdriver and used that! The gesture lent a touch of humor to a light and informal gathering. For some reason, though, no one's asked me to fetch a circle-casting tool since then . . .

A Wiccan Circle Casting

For this circle, we'll use the guided meditation technique introduced in the last chapter. The idea is to make an inner journey to a Celtic sacred site, to infuse your circle with energy from that place. The first few times you do this, you'll find that it seems to take many minutes. With practice, you'll be able to find that inner place easily and quickly.

When you and your ritual area are prepared, take a few minutes to ground the energies of your day. Your candle or other visual focus should be on your altar. When you have cleared your mind, stand before the altar, but about one step away from it. Knock three times upon your altar (or ring a bell three times) to signify the beginning of your rite. Take up your tool and hold it at the level of your heart. Close your eyes and breathe deeply.

Imagine that you are in a place of shadows. This is a mysterious place, but you are not frightened. You are here to begin a journey.

Step forward (in the physical realm) and make a Sign of Entering, a ritual posture (called "rending the veil" in ceremonial magic) like this: Reach out your arms in front of you, fingers together. Bring your arms together with the backs of your hands touching and the palms turned outward. If you are carrying an athame, hold it in the hand you use most. Draw the palms apart as if opening a curtain.

As you make the Sign of Entering, the mists and shadows seem to clear, and you find yourself in a green field surrounded by tall trees and a bank of earth. It is night, with a full moon shedding light. You are aware of birds and forest animals in the area. In the center of the field there is a stone well.

You approach the well, and find that the water is high enough for you to see the moon's reflection. This place, where the moonlight meets the water, is the site of a great mystery: the sacred triad of Land, Sea, and Sky meeting as one.

Reach out with both hands and touch the point of your athame to the surface of the water. As the ripples scatter the moon's reflection, feel a rush of moonlight pouring into your body and into the sacred knife you carry. Remain in this place for a moment, feeling the glowing moonlight infusing your outstretched hands.

Pull your hands back toward your heart as you take a step backward, then sweep your arms downward so that the point of your knife (or wand or fingertips) is aimed at a spot on the ground just below the center of your altar. Visualize the moonlight flowing forth from your instrument to inscribe a gleaming circle on the ground.

Continue to face outward as you move to the right around the circle, keeping the point focused on the perimeter.

When you reach the point at which you started, stand straight, pull your hands back toward your heart, then return your tool to the altar. While you remain in your circle, keep in your mind the visualization of a glowing boundary between you and the world, helping to focus your magic and keep out unwanted energies.

Taking Up the Circle

When you cast a circle, you usually "take it up" afterward, so as not to leave the ritual energy floating through someone's living space. (This also is simply a symmetrical way of ending the ritual, which is why we do it even outdoors.)

Even when it's positive, spiritual energy isn't always harmonious with daily living. And on those rare occasions when something goes wrong—well, have you ever been at a party where something went really wrong? Perhaps a couple had a bitter public fight, or the hostess's dog suddenly turned vicious? The energy of the room didn't feel right afterward, even when the problem went away, and you probably left as soon as possible. The same idea applies to the circle. Rituals take people beyond their normal spheres of existence, and the circle is one way to contain the energies of those spheres, so that if they are not what we want we can banish them from our space.

In taking up a circle, the practitioner sends those energies down into the earth, called "grounding." This is rather like grounding an electrical current—it doesn't pollute the earth, but simply neutralizes the energy. This process provides a transition back into ordinary life, and keeps the physical space magically "clean" for daily use. Here, we'll ground the circle we raised in the last section.

Return to the altar and stand in front of it. Take up your athame and hold it in both hands, close to your heart. Close your eyes and take a deep breath. When you are ready, sweep the blade downward, aimed at the starting point of your circle. Visualize the silver-white moonlight of the circle's perimeter flowing upward into the knife.

Step to the left and around the circle, "sweeping" the circle's light with your athame. Visualize the area around your hands growing brighter and brighter as you move around the circle, leaving darkness behind. When you return to the altar, stand straight and hold your hands to your heart as you close your eyes.

See yourself once more in the grove of ancient trees, dark and green and foreboding. Before you is the stone well, its surface calm and clearly reflecting the full moon above. Hold both hands in front of you, then slowly bring the point of your blade downward to just touch the surface of the water. Feel the glowing moonlight pour back into the water, the earth, and the sky.

Step back from the well, and bow in gratitude to the spirits of this place.

In the physical world, take a step backward and make a Closing Sign thus: Stretch your arms out to your sides, palms facing each other, athame in your dominant hand. Draw your hands together as if closing a pair of curtains (this is the opposite of the Sign of Entering you made at the beginning). As you do this, return your mind fully to the place where you are. Knock or ring a bell three times to signify the end of your rite.

Cutting a Door

Usually, once a circle is cast, the people within it expect to stay there for the duration of the ritual. Sometimes, though, someone needs to leave, whether as part of the ritual or to deal with an unexpected problem.

If this happens, use your athame to "cut a door" in a section between two quarter candles. To do this, bring the blade down at the right-hand edge of your door, so that the blade's flat section faces the perimeter of the circle. Sweep it along the circle for a few feet, and visualize the light of the circle being pushed to the left. When the person returns, face your athame's blade along the perimeter and "pull" the circle back to the right to recast the circle and close the door.

Of course, if a real emergency occurs, don't worry about cutting a door—just leave, or do whatever you have to do! Any magical disturbance in the room can be dealt with after the fire is put out or the person who fainted has been revived.

A Celtic Circle

This is the circle-casting ritual I use, based on a Druid rite written by Brendan Myers (Cathbad). The principle behind it is a little different from the Wiccan procedure outlined above. Instead of taking an inner journey to a place of power to gather energy for the protection of the circle, this rite honors and summons the spirits of nature, which are always present and available to you.

I use a wooden staff for this part of my rituals, as a way of acknowledging the importance of trees in Celtic mythology. Ash is the wood most commonly found in Celtic sacrificial wells and pits, and was considered powerful in that ancient world. My staff is not of ash, but of a tree significant to me, an apple tree that stood near my childhood home and which to me seemed to symbolize a refuge and the renewal of the seasons. During a difficult year in my adult life, the tree was felled by lightning. I took a long, straight piece of the wood as my staff to signify my own progress from childhood to adulthood, from that time of trouble to a happier life. Each time I use the staff, I honor the places and people of my own history.

If a staff is unavailable or inappropriate for your space, use a wand or tree branch (take it from a fallen limb if you can, rather than harming a living tree).

The nature principles honored here are those mentioned in an old Irish triad: Land, Sea, and Sky. The triad-poem cannot be traced any earlier than the medieval period, but these natural realms are known to have been sacred to the Celts.

Prepare yourself, your altar, and your ritual area, as in the previous example, and take a few moments to ground and center yourself in that space. When you are ready to begin, touch the staff to the ground three times and say:

Fruitful Land, support and uphold us with your powers of nur-turance, sustenance, and life. Blessed are we!

As you do this, visualize the bounty of the earth, which feeds us and gives form to our lives.

Next, hold the staff vertically in front of you in both hands and walk around the perimeter of your ritual area, saying:

Turbulent Sea, surround and protect us with your powers of cleansing, healing, and love. Blessed are we!

As you walk around, visualize your ritual area as an island, pro-tected on all sides by gently rolling waves.

Finally, lift the staff up toward the sky (be careful if you're work-ing in a room with low ceilings!):

Radiant Sky, guide and inspire us with your powers of light, free-dom, and wisdom. Blessed are we!

Pause a moment and gaze at the sky. If indoors, visualize the sky as it actually appears outside, whether it be dark or light, cloudy or clear. Turn to face the center and proclaim:

Thus the Realms make sacred our circle.

Set the staff down, perhaps resting it against a wall near the altar, then continue with your rite.

When you are ready to depart the circle, take up the staff once more. This part of the rite goes quickly, for the energies we have summoned are natural and ever present. They do not need to be dismissed or "taken up." All we need do is say farewell.

Hold the staff up to the sky:

Radiant Sky, we thank Thee for thy guidance, inspiration, and light, which are with us always. Hail and farewell!

Hold the staff vertically in front of you and proceed around the edge of the ritual area counterclockwise:

Turbulent Sea, we thank Thee for thy surrounding, cleansing, and protection, which are with us always. Hail and farewell!

Finally, touch the staff to the ground three times:

Fruitful Land, we thank Thee for thy nurturance, foundation, and renewal, which are with us always. Hail and farewell!

Turn to face the center and proclaim:

Thus with honor to the Realms we end our rite.

The Four Quarters

Very early in human history, people noticed that the sun always rose in roughly the same direction and set on the opposite side of the sky. The naming of east and west, north and south was often followed by the association of rituals and sacred purposes with these "quarters." The Greeks and Romans named the winds that blew from the four main compass directions, and honored those winds as messengers of the gods. This concept worked its way into medieval magic and thence to Wicca, where it has become a traditional part of rituals.

We have very little evidence indicating the Celts found one direction to be more sacred than another or associated with any particular quality. Many tombs from the Celtic era have their openings toward the east, but we don't know what that signified to the builders. East simply may have been the direction best sheltered from the wind.

In Wicca, once the circle is cast, one or more people summon magical guardians from each cardinal direction, usually starting in the east, and honor the energies, qualities, and symbols associated with that direction. Because of the independent-minded nature of Wiccans, there are many different sets of these correspondences. The following should be useful in most situations, but there are many possible systems.

East: Associated with the element Air, the powers of the mind, books, learning, communication, the color blue, the wand, incense, springtime, morning, insight, wisdom.

South: Associated with the element Fire, the powers of the will, strength, heat, light, the color red, the athame, candles, summer, midday, inspiration, passion.

West: Associated with the element Water, the powers of emotion, the color green, the chalice and water bowl, autumn, evening, rain, plants, love, healing.

North: Associated with the element Earth, the powers of stability, the physical world, yellows and browns, rocks, the pentacle, salt, winter, midnight, that which is enduring, form, foundation.

In some systems, each direction is said to have a "guardian" or "Watchtower." These are entities that are available in an unseen spiritual world (sometimes referred to simply as "the inner") to serve as guards of your circle. The concept of Watchtowers comes from ceremonial magic, but Wiccans have used it for decades, building up considerable energy around these entities. Unlike deities, the Watchtowers are not seen in human form, but often as glowing towers of light that can be summoned and dismissed by the practitioner. Think of them as neither male nor female, simply as extensions of your own personal power, drawing on the powers of nature and the work of those who came to the sacred circle in years past.

Not all Wiccans visualize the Watchtowers in this way; many prefer to simply "welcome" the "spirits" of the directions. I find my circles more powerful and my rituals more energized when the Watchtowers are invoked. You may wish to try several methods, or use different quarter calls in different situations.

Here, we'll call the Watchtowers using some imagery from Irish legend. A medieval text describes four sacred cities, Gorias, Murias, Findias, and Falias, as the homes of the Tuatha dé Danaan. The Tuatha are the "People of Danu" who are known now as Irish goddesses and gods. Many Celtic-oriented practitioners who are familiar with the Wiccan quarters invoke the four treasures of these sacred cities—a sword from which none could escape, a spear of certain victory, an inexhaustible cauldron of food, and a sacred stone that cried out under a true king—in the four directions. (The first Wiccans may have referred to this legend when choosing the four tools of Wicca.)

There is no evidence that the Irish envisioned these sacred cities in the four compass quadrants. The association of the cities with the four directions in this rite should be considered a nod to Wiccan tradition rather than an ancient custom.

To Call the Quarters

After your circle is cast, take up your wand if you have one, and proceed to the East. (See why you marked the directions with candles or stones?) Besides its unknown significance to Celtic tomb-builders, the direction of the sunrise is associated with beginnings in many traditions.

Lift your arms above your head. If you are carrying a wand, hold it horizontally in your dominant hand. If using your hands, hold them with palms outward. Raise the wand or your hands so as to form a boundary at the perimeter of your circle. With this gesture, you ask the guardian to stand outside your circle, to serve as a watcher rather than adding its energies within.

> *Guardian of the East*
> *Who comes from Gorias*
> *Keeper of the spear of Lugh*
> *I do summon thee*
> *From the morning lands*
> *To attend this place of magic*
> *As a guard and witness.*
> *As I will, so mote it be!*

("Mote" is a Wiccan archaicism, a word added to modern rituals to make them sound old. It means "must" or "shall.")

Visualize the tower of light appearing outside the circle to answer your call. Now move around the circle clockwise to the other three points, and repeat the process three more times.

Guardian of the South
Who comes from Findias
Keeper of the sword of Nuada
I do summon thee
From the sunlit lands
To attend this place of magic
As a guard and witness.
As I will, so mote it be!

Guardian of the West
Who comes from Murias
Keeper of the cauldron of the Dagda
I do summon thee
From the misty lands
To attend this place of magic
As a guard and witness.
As I will, so mote it be!

Guardian of the North
Who comes from Falias
Keeper of Lia Fail, the Stone of Sovereignty,
I do summon thee
From the midnight mountains
To attend this place of magic
As a guard and witness.
As I will, so mote it be!

At the end of the ritual, you'll dismiss the four guardians. As with the circle casting, this is a matter of returning energies to their proper sphere, and thus goes rather quickly. Stand in the North in the same "boundary" position you assumed before:

Guardian of the North
I thank you
For your presence and protection
And bid you
Hail and Farewell!

Visualize the Watchtower fading back to darkness. Repeat in the other directions, moving counterclockwise, ending in the East.

Ordinarily, the Watchtowers are invoked at the beginning and end of the ritual, but are not referred to otherwise. You may find occasionally that they make their presence known through the candles in the four directions. For example, when participants direct energy toward a certain place outside the circle, the candle in that direction may flicker in response.

The circle is a protected place, a platform from which we can venture into the inner realms. After some practice, the mere act of casting a circle will help you to leave behind the details of daily life and prepare to use your personal magical power. For those who aren't used to such work, I suggest practicing for five days by casting a circle and calling the quarters. Meditate within your space, then dismiss the Watchtowers and take up the circle. Repeat this exercise whenever you have spent more than a month away from your spiritual work.

By the end of this period you should be growing comfortable with these actions. Decide on a standard ritual opening and closing formula, true to your goals and suited to your needs. Become familiar with these until you can do them easily from memory, so you can concentrate on magic and worship.

Celtic Gods and Goddesses

In the past couple of chapters, we've discussed meditation, visualization, and ritual. When used in combination with your own personal power, these are great techniques for growth and learning. In this chapter, we'll use those same techniques to admit a much higher power into our lives through worship of a goddess or god.

There are literally hundreds of Celtic deities whose names are known today. To get you started, here are brief profiles of seven Celtic deities, plus a final goddess who is widely perceived as Celtic but was unknown in ancient times.

For each deity, I've written a spell or ritual, illustrating some of the common Wiccan techniques for forging a connection with a god or goddess. This connection is the most powerful part of Wiccan ritual—the chance to use your own energy in worship and devotion, and to partake of divine guidance and inspiration. The spells are written for a solitary practitioner, but can be easily adapted for a small group, or for any other needs. Lastly, each section offers some suggestions for embodying divine energies in your daily life and in your community.

Through ritual, Wiccans build and intensify their relationships with their goddesses and gods. Instead of just saying their prayers, Wiccans create a sacred space and then invite their deities to visit it. Often, practitioners do spellwork to solve their own problems, asking the deities to bless their rituals and intentions. In other situations, Wiccans may enter a meditative state, asking the goddess or god to inspire them with guidance or prophecy.

Invoking a deity requires some preparation. Gods and goddesses are powerful beings, and their energy is best experienced within a cast circle. Before invoking a goddess or god, get yourself and your ritual space ready for the presence of the divine. Set up your altar, arrange appropriate music and scents, put on your ritual clothing. Thoroughly "ground and center"—that is, spend a few minutes in meditation, perhaps doing the Tree Meditation, to put aside the emotions of your day and offer your worship in the clearest possible frame of mind. Then perform whatever ritual opening you choose.

Before you begin to close down your circle, offer a pinch of incense or a little wine or juice to the deities you have invoked (the liquid can be poured out on the ground in libation later). Thank them for their presence, and for any guidance or energy they have given to you during the ritual. Then bid them "Hail and farewell," and perform your standard ritual closing.

Don't try to form connections with all of these gods and goddesses at once. Instead, read through this chapter and pick one or two that seem to attract or "fit" you in some way. Some may become part of your daily worship, while others remain simply figures of history to you.

Brigid

In History: In "Cormac's Glossary," a compendium of Irish myth written down by a Christian around 900 c.e., Brigid is described as three goddesses of the same name, one a patroness of learning, one of healing, and one of smithcraft. The name Brigid is said to come from a word meaning "exalted one." Such a title could be applied to any deity, which may explain the many aspects attached to her name.

Brigid is also the name of a Christian saint, St. Bridget, who lived in the fifth century C.E. Because her life is not well documented, mythology has added the qualities of the goddess to those of the living woman. A perpetual flame was kept burning for centuries at Kildare in honor of Bridget, who founded an order of nuns there, and even skeptical scholars admit the possibility that this flame dates back to Pagan tradition.

Besides flames, she is associated in Christian and Pagan myth with fertility. The goddess Brigid is said to have been invoked in childbirth; St. Bridget is said to have access to endless supplies of food, milk, and ale. The feast day of the saint is February 1, the Pagan festival of Imbolc, which may be in part a celebration of the first milk of the ewe. Finally, many wells and several rivers in England and Scotland were named after Brigid, indicating her association with water.

In Modern Worship: Many Wiccans are drawn to Brigid, and it is no wonder, for her blessings are the things that help us live instead of merely surviving. She has the power to heal illness and take away pain. Hers also are poetry, learning, and the creative arts. And the fires of her forge perform a magic known to all metalworkers—the magic that takes something rough and unformed, subjects it to heat and stress, and brings it out stronger, brighter, and more powerful. For some, this magic takes the form of metalcraft, making anything from knives to jewelry. For others, Brigid's forge is a metaphor for any act of transformation.

Brigid is most often celebrated at the festival of Imbolc, when the bright fires of her worship are a welcome antidote to short, gray days and long, cold nights. This time of year, when nature seems mostly dormant, is also related to her aspect of fertility, for it is then that the green and growing forces of nature lie still. Science tells us that many people become mildly depressed at this time of year. With her flame and her promise, Brigid gives us hope that the light will return.

A Brigid Spell: Do this when you have need of any of Brigid's aspects, or to start or strengthen a relationship with her.

Place three votive candles on a metal or ceramic plate. The candles can be white, but fiery colors (red, orange, yellow, gold) are also appropriate. Also have ready a metal object such as a non-sacred knife, letter opener or pen; you will use this to carve symbols on the candles.

Prepare for ritual, and then perform your standard opening ceremony. When you are ready, stand before your altar and invoke Brigid by repeating this poem three times:

> Wisdom of the water
> Passion of the flame
> Abundance of the green earth
> Brigid, I call thy name.

Light one of the candles and say:

> Goddess of healing,
> Enter into my body
> Enter into my mind
> Enter into my life
> Help me to shed that which has held me back.
> Help me to use my strength for thy honor,
> And for the good of all.

Offer your own personal prayers for healing. (For more about prayers for the healing of others, see the Ethics section.) Visualize yourself as healthy and strong, partaking of Brigid's endless supply of energy and sustenance.

Now light the second candle and say:

> Goddess of smithcraft,
> Temper me in thy forge.
> Help me to use the resources of thy land
> With wisdom and honor, for the good of all.

Offer your prayers for projects in the physical world. Anything to do with metalworking qualifies, but this aspect of Brigid can also bless crafts (especially metal-related ones), jobs involving machinery, household improvements, and even car repairs. Visualize yourself as completing these works successfully, managing your energy and learning by doing.

Now light the third candle and say:

> *Goddess of poetry,*
> *Bless my creativity.*
> *Help me to cast aside fear and constriction*
> *Help me to be as thy poets of old,*
> *A speaker of what is and is not.*
> *Help me to bring forth beauty and truth.*

Offer your prayers for creative projects. Music, writing, painting, and sculpture are creative—but so is taking on a charity project, tending a garden, or refinishing a bookshelf. If you feel your life lacks a creative aspect, ask Brigid to show you the way toward one. Visualize yourself as fearless and contented in your creative life, overflowing with inspiration.

Remain in meditation on the three aspects of Brigid for a few moments. Think about how these three elements find their own balance in your life.

When you are ready to leave the circle, stand before the altar once more. Take up the knife or pen and blow out the candle of Healing. Then, as the wax cools, carve a personal symbol of healing on the candle. This may represent overcoming a specific illness. For instance, I have trouble with tendinitis in my ankles, so my healing candle bears the symbol of a confidently striding figure. Or it may represent general health and well-being. You might even just write the word "Healing" on the candle.

Replace the healing candle, and blow out the candle of Smith-craft. This symbol should come more easily, since its manifestations are so physical in nature. A symbol of the completed project you are working on, whether you're making a ritual knife or building a garage, would be most appropriate. If you do not have any particular goal in this area of life, you might draw a symbol of a real-world skill you wish to acquire.

Now take up the third candle, that of Poetry. This symbol is the most personal of all, and you may wish to spend a moment or two in contemplation, or ask Brigid to show you how best to represent your own creativity.

When you are finished, bid farewell to the goddess:

Healing Mother,
Goddess of the Forge,
Inspiration of the Bards
I thank you for your blessings and protection.
I take with me these symbols of your flame,
To bring you close when I have need.
Hail and farewell!

Close your circle. Light each of the three candles at a time when you are concentrating on that area of your life. For instance, you might light the Healing candle when you are feeling unwell, or before an appointment with a doctor or therapist. If it is safe to do so, keep the Smithcraft candle lit in your work area when focusing on a new craft or skill, or light it in thanks when a handcrafted project is completed. Light the Poetry candle when expressing your own beauty and truth, particularly when trying a new form of creative expression.

Brigid in Daily Life: You manifest the qualities of this goddess when you act in ways that are healing to yourself or others. Listening to a troubled friend can be an act of healing—but so can protecting your own well-being by asking someone in need of counseling to get professional help. Exercise, particularly outdoors, evokes Brigid's healing qualities.

Brigid's flame also burns bright when you transform raw material into something refined, strong, and beautiful. Brigid's smithcraft is active and physical. Forging metal requires a great deal of skill, and you bring Brigid's fire into the world when you learn new skills, practice and improve the ones in which you are experienced, and teach them to others.

Finally, beyond mere creative release, Brigid's poetic aspect is a force for truth. The bards of old were the historians, journalists, and critics of their society, praising leaders who succeeded and satirizing those who failed. Practicing creative arts is one way of manifesting this aspect. (For more on this, see the chapter on the Celtic Creative Tradition.) Another way to express this side of Brigid's energy is to speak in ways that will lead to building a better world. Do not merely dwell in your community, but participate by voting, learning about the issues and systems that surround you, and using your voice to make things better.

Lugh

In History: The stories of Lugh (pronounced "Loog" or "Lou," and also known as Llew, Lugos, or Lugus) are known only from the Christian era, with the earliest dating perhaps to the ninth or tenth centuries C.E. But his name was known much earlier. There are a number of places in the ancient world that derive their names from his, or from some common word root (scholar Alexei Kondratiev suggests it might have meant "illumination" or "lightning"). Perhaps the best known of these places is the city known to the Romans as Lugdunum, which survives as the French city of Lyons. The English city of Carlisle also takes its ancient name, Luguvallium, from the same source.

Unlike many Celtic deities, his name is known across a wide range of territory, perhaps because he was associated with trade. In the Roman period, his qualities (skill, craftsmanship, prosperity, and trickery) were ascribed to Mercury, and some of the figures usually thought of as depicting the Roman god Mercury may have been statues of Lugh.

In early Irish literature, Lugh is a mighty spearman, a magician who can influence the outcomes of battles. As the father of the hero Cú Chulainn, he makes a magical appearance on the battlefield, holds off the enemy so his son can get some sleep, and heals the sleeping champion's wounds. Historian Anne Ross traces Lugh's association with ravens and eagles, and suggests also an association with dogs or wolves.

Lugh is most often celebrated at the festival that bears his name, Lughnasadh (sometimes called by the Christian name of Lammas, perhaps because it's easier to spell and pronounce). It is held on or about August 1, and is traditionally a time to celebrate the first fruits of the year's harvest. This might have been a time for fairs, markets, contests, even military campaigns—anything that brought people together during good traveling weather. Thus Lugh, with his many skills, became associated with trade and commerce as well as the skills of a good warrior.

In Modern Worship: Lugh's festival is at the opposite season from Brigid's, and his qualities in many ways complement hers. Where she provides the energy and inspiration, Lugh provides the skill and resources. The seeds prepared in winter become the harvest that Lugh inaugurates. Many Wiccans invoke Lugh as a sky god, and ask his blessings on their gardens.

Lughnasadh is still prime traveling season for many, and Northern-Hemisphere Wiccans often travel to festivals or large group rituals at this time of year. This provides an opportunity to meet new people, exchange news, show off their creative achievements, and partake of the energy of group rituals. In some Wiccan cosmologies, the god "dies" every year at this time, sacrificing himself for the harvest, to be reborn in winter.

Lugh is an excellent deity for this age of multitasking. One of his descriptive names is Samildanach, "the Many-Skilled," and those of us who have complicated lives may take inspiration from his profusion of abilities. In the story of the second battle of Mag Tuireadh, he comes to the door of Nuada, the king, and is refused admittance unless he has "an art." In turn he offers his skills as wright, smith, champion, harper, poet, historian, sorcerer, cupbearer, and more. Call on Lugh when life forces you to balance many things at once.

In the same story, Lugh then pulls together the talents of the various gods, craftsmen, sorcerers, and warriors gathered to fight the

Fomorians, asking each one what he can do to help in the battle. Lugh is not only a god, but also a king—a true leader who can bring out the best in the people who surround him. His wisdom can help show you how to rally people around a common goal.

A Rite of Lugh: In this ritual you'll call on Lugh's association with hands and skill to make a spell you can use any time you have need of his qualities.

Find a place, indoors or out, where you can be reasonably private. You'll need some paper (parchment is nice if you can get it) and pen, markers or paint, plus a ribbon or piece of leather.

Cast your circle by walking around it three times "deosil," repeating this chant:

> *Magic of Lugh, protect this circle*
> *Strength of Lugh, inspire my work*
> *Light of Lugh, inspire my words*

Walk around the perimeter of the circle to each direction in turn, starting with east and using the following invocations:

> *Guardian of the East, guard this circle with thy winds of insight.*
> *Guardian of the South, guard this circle with thy fire of might and passion.*
> *Guardian of the West, guard this circle with thy oceans of mystery.*
> *Guardian of the North, guard this circle with thy hard unbending stone.*

Stand before your altar and close your eyes as you invoke Lugh:

> *Lugh who shines in skies of gold*
> *Lugh Lámhfhada, Skillful Hand*
> *Come and be worshiped, god of old,*
> *whose Lightning flashes over the land.*
> *Hail, brilliant god!*

Breathe deeply, feeling the spirit of Lugh permeating your circle. Then open your eyes and set some incense alight.

God of the harvest,
I make offering to you.
I pray for fruitfulness,
That my efforts may yield prosperity
To myself and those around me.
God of many skills,
I make offering to you.
I pray for craftsmanship
That my work may be useful and beautiful.
God and King of the Tuatha dé Danaan,
I make offering to you.
I pray for my community
May the best of my abilities
Be honorably and freely given
To the people I call my own.

Place the paper on a flat surface, and on it place the hand you use most often. Trace the outline of this hand with your pen, markers, or paint. This will require concentration, since you're probably not used to working with the other hand! Once you've got the outline, remove your hand and decorate the outline with words and images associated with the skills you want to develop.

When you are finished, remain in meditation for a few minutes. If you have a specific question or problem, focus on it for a few moments, then move it to the back of your mind. If images or words float into your mind, remember them, but do not dwell on them just now. Remain open to new messages.

Save the hand-drawing and roll it into a scroll (this can wait till after the ritual if it isn't dry). Tie it with the ribbon or leather.

Offer your thanks to Lugh.

God of Lightning, all honor to thee!

Dismiss each compass direction, starting in the North:

Guardian of the North (West, South, East), I thank you and bid you farewell.

Now walk counterclockwise around your circle, visualizing its magical energy dissipating into rays of light. Put the scroll near a practical space where your skills are required—perhaps your computer desk, art space, workshop or even your car—or burn it when your problem is resolved or your goal accomplished.

Lugh in Daily Life: Lugh is associated with the harvest, which makes gardening a natural way to honor him. Even planting a few herbs in a window box, and watching their tiny leaves spring into life, brings Lugh's spirit into your world. Give thanks to him when you harvest the fruits of your labor. At work, Lugh's energy helps you perform well at tasks that require skill. Lugh teaches us to experience each task as a craft, worthy of study and effort.

Lugh brings together a group to work toward a common goal, whether it be fighting a war or harvesting a crop. Remember him when you are called upon to lead others, or when you hope to enlist the energies of others toward a community project.

In war, Lugh made sure to find out each person's talents and use them. When Lugh's son Cú Chulainn was weary with fighting, Lugh gave him an opportunity to sleep. Leaders watch out for the people on their team, and find ways to keep each person from getting drained. Their job is to fit everyone's talents together in a strategy that makes the most of the energy and skills available. Like Lugh, they work toward a goal, not toward their own glory. Their greatest joy is in seeing others succeed.

Epona

In History: Epona (pronounced "Eh-POE-na" or "Eh-PAW-na") holds the distinction of being the only Celtic deity formally adopted into the Roman pantheon. The Romans gave her the feast day of December 18, which may or may not reflect a Celtic celebration. Her name means "horse," and she is almost always depicted either on or beside a horse. She was widely worshiped across Europe, particularly by Celtic tribes known for their horsemanship.

Horses, of course, were highly valuable in the Celtic world. A horse could help its owner travel farther, trade over a larger area, fight battles more effectively, and perform heavier labor than mere human power could manage. A full stable indicated the owner's prosperity. Horses came to symbolize wealth and status, and are depicted on many Celtic coins. The Celts admired horses' beauty and strength, and frequently used equine themes in their art.

In two ancient statues Epona holds keys, which may be keys to a stable but may also have an otherworldly meaning. Her image was sometimes carved on gravestones, perhaps reflecting an ancient belief in a horse that carries the dead to the next world. She is associated with death, but also with the fruits of the earth, which she feeds to the animals and birds that surround her.

Epona's cult grew more popular as Celtic tribes' military operations grew more dependent on cavalry. At least one scholar suggests that warriors on horseback were the elite of their society, the class from which kings were drawn. If this is true, it helps explain Epona's widespread worship. Her adoption into the state religion of Rome reflects the empire's dependence on horses for war and trade.

This association of horses with Celtic peoples continues to the present day, for Great Britain and Ireland are home to breeders whose horses are famous worldwide.

In Modern Worship: Epona is, as you might expect, most popular among those Wiccans who love horses. Horse owners experience Epona's essence every day as they care for and enjoy their animals. Some of her ancient statues also show the goddess with dogs, snakes, and birds, and today she is invoked for nurturance and protection of all domestic animals.

One of the first Wiccan spells I ever read invoked Epona for protection of a car! Our vehicles, while not living beings, offer us some of the same experiences as a horse would have to an ancient Celt. They give us freedom to travel and a wider range of work opportunities; they require care and "feeding"; they serve as symbols of our wealth. Protection of a car is a perfectly valid object of spellwork.

One of Epona's greatest lessons is this: Every blessing brings with it a responsibility. The stewardship of an animal's life is an obvious example. In the right circumstances, horses and dogs can still provide practical benefits to a household, and even the smallest pets provide companionship and enjoyment. Yet "owning" an animal carries with it the moral obligation to care for it, and Wiccans, like most people in Western culture, reserve some of their sharpest disdain for people who disregard this responsibility.

Likewise, those who are blessed with great wealth have the responsibility of safeguarding their riches. The more ethical among them also take on the responsibility of using their wealth for the greater good. If you are blessed with a fulfilling love, you are responsible for keeping it alive by showing your affection and behaving ethically toward your partner. Children are a vast responsibility, and one of the rewards of parenthood is teaching sons and daughters the best uses of the blessings they enjoy. Whatever your blessings, you will enjoy them longer and more fully if you can recognize and live up to their attendant responsibilities.

An Epona Spell: Before you start, it will help to find a way to spend some time around real horses. This needn't be a mystical experience; I was able to gain valuable lessons simply by visiting a friend who owns horses. Paying my respects to those animals, feeding them apples and getting to know their personalities, helped open my spirit to the goddess who protects them.

If you don't know anyone who has horses, you might enjoy calling a local stable for a trail ride, or visiting a horse show or horse race. If there's no way you can spend time with real horses, try reading books or watching films in which horses are depicted realistically and play a central role.

Next, you'll need a talisman (that is, a small object that will carry magical power). It should be one that evokes Epona's essence in your own mind. A horse-shaped pendant or charm would be one example, or a small horse molded from clay. I chose to use an old key, one I no longer needed, to reflect Epona's association with keys.

If you have any animals in your household, you may want to make them part of your circle for this ritual. Pets should be allowed to enter and leave the circle freely. Like small children, they usually do not disturb the magical boundary when they cross it. If your animals don't have the run of the house, perform the ritual in the barn or stable, or near the aquarium. It may be a little disorienting at first, but the animals' presence will help to evoke the energies of Epona.

As part of your preparations, make some food available to the animals during the ceremony. Then place a small amount of the food in a dish on the altar. Feel free to take time out during this ritual to interact with your animals, petting them, talking with them or caring for their needs.

If you have no animals, find or make a picture or statue of a horse for your altar. Decorate your ritual area with pictures of animals you like. Instead of pet food, place an apple or some carrots on your altar, or perhaps a dish of birdseed.

Prepare your circle and yourself for ritual. Place your talisman on the altar, and ground and center. When you have cast and guarded the circle according to your custom, invoke Epona with the following words:

> Mother of animals, keeper of keys,
> Epona, Great Queen, I call to thee.
> Guardian of horses strong and free,
> Epona, Great Queen, I worship thee.
> Thine are the blessings of liberty,
> Thine are the gifts of beauty and grace,
> And whenever I ask a blessing of thee,
> Its burdens I do fully embrace.

Hold your talisman in your hand. As you handle it, investing it with your personal energy, choose a part of your life in which you seek Epona's prosperity and protection. This may be a gift you already enjoy and wish to safeguard, or it may be something new you desire. Visualize yourself delighting in the rewards of this gift, deriving joy and energy from it.

Now visualize yourself taking proper care of this gift. If you seek love, picture yourself acting in loving ways, spending time to ensure that your relationship lasts. If you seek a better job, picture yourself doing extra work or studying new skills to be a valued employee. If you seek to develop a talent, picture yourself using that ability to help others.

Return once more to the first visualization, of yourself enjoying the benefits of your gift. Realize that those benefits will be sweeter and the rewards more meaningful because of the energy you have invested. Remain a few moments in contemplation of this dual vision. Then, in your own words, ask Epona to bless your talisman, and ask her for the gift you seek. In this sacred moment, make a specific promise to Epona of the things you will do to safeguard and care for your gift.

Be still for a few moments, listening. The pictures and words that come into your mind at this time may have meaning within the context of this ritual. Remember them, but do not try to analyze them now. Just listen.

When you are ready to end the ritual, put your talisman somewhere on your person, either placing it in a pocket or tying it with a cord to wear around your neck. Lift up the food from the altar and offer your thanks to the goddess:

> Epona, Mother Goddess, I celebrate thee.
> Through thy power I am set free
> Through thy care I guard my treasures
> For thee I carry my burdens with pleasure.
> I ask thy blessings on house and coffer
> And to thy creatures this gift I offer.

Close the circle according to your custom. Give the small dish of food to your animals, or make sure your food offering is somehow otherwise shared with animals. Keep the talisman to remind you of your wish and your promise.

Epona in Daily Life: As I've mentioned, some modern Wiccans call on Epona to protect their vehicles. I make a habit of silently giving thanks to Epona for protecting me and my vehicle whenever I emerge safely from bad weather, avoid a speed trap, or pass by an accident. I'm not going to make any promises about the effectiveness of this, but a few years ago I stopped doing it—and immediately got three speeding tickets. Epona got my attention once more.

Of course, it may be that thinking of Epona focuses my mind on driving more safely. But the gods of Wicca often grant benefits in this way, by moving us to make our own luck. To gain this protection for your vehicle, make an Epona talisman with the spell above and hang it on your rear view mirror. Remember to thank the goddess when you get safely through a risky situation.

In her role as keeper of the keys, Epona acts as guardian of that which we most cherish. Another good place for her protective talismans is over the door to your home or bedroom, or in the box where you keep your most treasured possessions.

Finally, embody Epona's spirit by helping your local animal shelter with donations of food, money, or volunteer time; taking good care of the animals in your home, and willingly shouldering the responsibilities that come with every blessing you enjoy.

Cernunnos

In History: The name Cernunnos is written on just one ancient depiction of the god—and even then, we can't be sure the first letter is a C. Another dedication from the Roman era (when, as noted earlier, the names of Roman and Celtic gods were often combined) honors "Jupiter Cernenus." On this slim evidence the forest-god is dubbed Cernunnos (usually pronounced "Kair-NOO-nohs") in modern writings about Celtic religion. It's quite possible that the same type of god was worshiped under many names. Later British folklore describes a hunter-god Herne, who may be related to this archetype.

By whatever name, this horned god was very popular. Most commonly, he is associated with the stag, and the god is shown wearing stag's antlers. He is often shown seated cross-legged, and usually has a beard and a *torc* (the neck ornament of the Celts, an almost-circle of metal ending in front in two decorated knobs). Frequently, Celtic worshipers associated him with the sun, and he is shown holding a wheel symbolizing the sun's rays. Another association is the ram-headed serpent, a very ancient Celtic symbol drawing on the power associated with horned beasts.

Some writers studying the ancient Celtic world have dubbed him "Lord of the Animals," for the stag-god is frequently given a place of prominence among various beasts. A relief from Reims, France, shows him attended by two classical gods, Mercury and Apollo, perhaps a testament to his enduring power in a time of increasing Romanization. He is gazing benevolently at a bull and stag below him, while a purse in his hands pours forth money. Archaeologist Miranda Green suggests that the rat portrayed above him may indicate an underworld aspect to his worship.

The stag-god was a god of hunting, and some depictions show this directly by giving him a club or spear. Because successful hunting brought food and comfort to a tribe, he is also associated with prosperity. Besides coins, he is sometimes shown with cornucopias, the "horns of plenty" that are an ancient symbol of material well-being. The Celts saw no conflict between a god of hunters and a god of beasts who were often hunted, and the ritual below explores this dual aspect.

As Christianity spread through the Celtic lands, the figure of the horned god came to represent the forces of evil, and eventually was transformed into "the devil." Why this god, and not the other Celtic deities? Perhaps because of his popularity, or because his well-known physical attributes (horns, beard, squatting posture, association with cloven-hoofed animals) made him easy to satirize.

In Modern Worship: Cernunnos is among the best-known gods worshiped by today's Wiccans, thanks to the work of anthropologist Margaret Murray, whose work inspired Gerald Gardner and the early Wiccans. Her theory of a horned "god of the witches," supposedly worshiped through the centuries, was swiftly discredited by scholars, but remained active for decades in the popular imagination. In 1957, Doreen Valiente was practicing with a coven that had grown apart from Gardner. This group's rituals sanctified the circle in the names of Aradia—an Italian goddess known not from history but from an 1898 book by an Englishman who claimed to have received the secrets of Italian witchcraft—and Cernunnos.

Perhaps because of this early start, Cernunnos is frequently invoked in Wiccan rituals, and is usually included when a list of gods' names is used in ritual. By "Cernunnos," Wiccans are usually referring to a generic Horned God who combines many of the elements of the stag-god and other horned gods—power among animals, masculine strength and sexuality, prosperity and victory. He is seen as a mysterious forest-god, whose essence can sometimes be experienced through rituals involving taking on the persona of a stag or other horned animal. Though the stag-god was very rarely shown with a consort, Cernunnos is frequently coupled in modern practice with a goddess, who may or may not be of Celtic origin.

Like Epona, he is associated with animals. Unlike her, he is more connected to wild creatures than to domestic ones. Many Wiccans turn to him when they begin exploring the essence of the divine male. Though he may be worshiped in an urban room lit by electricity and heated by fossil fuels, there is still in this god something of the wild forest hunter.

A Cernunnos Ritual: This guided meditation is intended to bring you closer to the essence of this god, and bring away a tool of personal power.

This rite involves hunting imagery. On the subject of hunting, as on most subjects, Wiccans' opinions vary. Some would not dream of hunting down the sacred creatures of nature, while others believe that a knowledgeable hunter providing food for his or her family is carrying out a fundamental ritual of the Pagan gods. Both of these views are perfectly acceptable—it's just one of the things on which many of us agree to disagree. Just as the hunt was vital to the well-being of a Celtic tribe, its spiritual aspect is vital to understanding Cernunnos.

To start, you will need a symbolic weapon. This needn't be large or elaborate; I used a small stone pendant shaped like an arrow.

Even a pointed stone would do, or a small stick with the point sharpened. Several Celtic excavations have uncovered ritual shafts in which worshipers offered miniature versions of real weapons as gifts to the gods. If the subject of weaponry interests you, you may wish to try to craft a small replica of a Celtic sword or spear out of wood, metal, clay, or bone.

If you can go to a forest to perform this ritual, so much the better. If this is impractical, try to surround your ritual space with evergreen branches, tree images, and forest sounds. Images of Cernunnos or the Green Man—a leaf-faced figure often found depicted in medieval churches, probably depicting a lost soul, but often transformed in modern Wiccan and Pagan practice into a forest-god—are also appropriate, as is evergreen-scented incense or oil.

When you have prepared yourself and your ritual space, place your symbolic weapon upon the altar. Prepare also a chalice or cup of cold water, which will serve to connect you to the physical world amid intense meditative work.

Breathe the scents of the forest as you ground and center. As you create your sacred circle, visualize your space surrounded by tall, dark trees. Cast your circle and call the quarters according to the method you prefer. (The Celtic circle casting given in the last chapter would be particularly appropriate here.) Then stand before the altar and hold your symbolic weapon in both hands as you invoke the god:

> *Cernunnos the Mighty, thou art the gray mist*
> *Cernunnos, thou art the forests of green*
> *Cernunnos, Lord of the creatures of earth*
> *In thee is the sacred victory seen.*
> *Cernunnos! Cernunnos! Cernunnos!*

Stand in meditation, visualizing before you the figure of a horned warrior. He may seem frightening or foreign, but you should not be afraid. He may appear sitting cross-legged on the ground or on an altar, and is frequently joined by one or more animals.

Hold out your symbolic weapon to him:

· Cernunnos, ancient god,
Accept this gift in thy honor
May my actions be swift and true
As the arrow of the hunter.

Remain in meditation for a moment, concentrating on the forest surrounding you. Hold your sacred weapon in your dominant hand (for most people, the right), with the point facing outward and your arm extended. Turn slowly all the way around, noticing where your weapon is pointed, as you repeat:

I am the hunter!

In your mind, try to fully enter into the mind of a hunter of old, killing not for joy but for survival. Use all the intelligence and knowledge at your command to track your prey, becoming at one with the forest surroundings, perhaps wearing the skin of a deer to disguise your scent. You may find yourself walking or running about your circle, or sitting in silent readiness. Take some time to experience this mental state.

Let your unconscious, guided by the god you have invoked, show you the end of the hunt. Perhaps you merely glimpse the prey and are left hungry and unsuccessful. Perhaps your weapon shoots home, and you experience the smells and sights of the bloody conclusion, and the knowledge that you have sustained the life of your tribe.

Remain in this visualization for several minutes. When you are ready, return to yourself and to the place where you are. Take a drink from the chalice of water.

If you wish to do the second part of this rite at this time, take a moment to ground and center. Otherwise, you may choose to end the ritual here, after thanking the god, and perform the next part on another occasion.

Put your symbolic weapon in your non-dominant hand, with the point facing toward yourself. Take a few steps backward, and with each one repeat:

I am the hunted!

Visualize yourself as a forest animal, the target of hunters. You can be any animal; choose one of whom you have some knowledge and feel some understanding.

What do you do to preserve your life? This depends largely on the nature of the animal you have chosen. Perhaps you remain perfectly still, trusting the wind to carry your scent away. Perhaps you flee pell-mell, or plot a careful strategy to disguise your flight. As prey, you must think on your feet, drawing on your knowledge of the land and on your own strengths and defenses.

Take some time to experience the sensations of this situation. What strengths do you find you have, when the emergency creates a need? These are the gifts of Cernunnos.

This time, do not let your unconscious decide the outcome. Decide that you will escape from the hunters, and visualize yourself doing so. (Why do I not recommend that you allow yourself to experience the death of the prey? First, because I believe death is an unknowable experience. Second, because the ritual enactment of a death can in my experience lead to tragic consequences for the one who takes on this role.)

When you are ready, return to this world and place your sacred weapon on the altar. Take a drink from the chalice of water. Then take your weapon in both hands and offer it to Cernunnos once more.

> *Cernunnos, Forest King*
> *Thy mystery is great*
> *Thou art the Hunter*
> *With courage and strength*
> *And the Hunted*
> *With swift intelligence*
> *Thou art both.*
> *I offer this weapon to thy service.*
> *Hail and farewell!*

End your ritual according to your practice. Be sure to ground and center thoroughly.

If you wish to embody the energies of Cernunnos in some part of your daily life, you may want to carry your symbolic weapon with you, or fashion it into a piece of jewelry. Otherwise, offer it to Cernunnos by burying it in a wooded place.

Cernunnos in Daily Life: The energy of Cernunnos is valuable in many situations. As a hunter god, his lessons include those of self-control—not repressing your anger or power, but channeling it productively to achieve your goals. As god of forest animals, he offers protection and helps avert danger. I sometimes wear a Cernunnos pendant at work when I wish to be "invisible," attracting no attention from those who might pile on more work or aggravation. But I also wear it when I wish to use my own power to achieve a goal that is truly mine.

Call on Cernunnos' abundant energy for situations when you need to manifest strength, cunning, or strategy. He is strongly tied to nature; I have called upon him to bless the land where I live, which is largely wooded.

Those who hunt, of course, will often feel some strong connection to Cernunnos. So will those who draw strength and renewal from simply walking in the woods. If you seek him, do so among trees, perhaps by a stream. If you seek to manifest his energy in the world, learn more about the forest environments closest to you, give money or time to groups that preserve forest land, plant trees on your own land, recycle paper and wood, or buy recycled tree products.

Rosmerta

In History: Rosmerta is best known for those statues in which she appears with the Roman god Mercury, as half of a divine couple. During the Romano-Celtic period, such pairings were a common way of introducing the new religion without asking people to give up their old deities. Mercury and Rosmerta were a well-known divine couple. Yet Rosmerta ("Rose-MUR-ta" or "Rose-MARE-ta") was no mere appendage, for she is also honored in statuary as a sole deity, sometimes linked with emperors. Even with her Roman counterpart, she is portrayed as an equal partner.

Her name means "Great Provider," and both alone and with Mercury she is a goddess of prosperity. She is often depicted with such wealth-related items as livestock, a bucket or cauldron (which symbolized plenty), a bag of coins, or a ship's rudder.

In Modern Worship: As in days of old, Rosmerta is sometimes invoked with Mercury and sometimes alone. Her name can be employed in prosperity rituals, and by those seeking success in business dealings, job applications, and court cases. Those seeking to have children also invoke her as a fertility goddess. Rosmerta is not one of the best-known Celtic goddesses, but her worship rewards the practitioner with warmth and benevolence.

In her role as partner with Mercury, she can be invoked to aid those who must stretch across the divides of different backgrounds to form productive alliances—a blended family, perhaps, or a Pagan organization.

In the next spell, we'll call on Rosmerta to bless a stable, loving partnership as one form of prosperity. This is not a known aspect of her ancient worship, but one based on a modern Wiccan observation of the ways in which she was depicted in history.

While many deities in the Celtic pantheon had sexual aspects, the Celts didn't have a god or goddess of love like the Roman Venus or Greek Aphrodite. Nor do we know much about the ways the Celts understood love or marriage, though evidence suggests Celtic women may have had somewhat greater freedom of choosing partners than women in other ancient societies.

The first written compilations of Irish law weren't made until the seventh or eighth century, but they are still widely perceived as reflecting some aspects of the Celtic culture. Interestingly, they specifically link marriage and prosperity, distinguishing between different types of marriage depending on which of the parties brought more property to it.

Today, the relationship between prosperity and partnership is still strong, though sometimes unacknowledged. This isn't about marrying for money. Simply, a stable relationship helps ensure greater security for both partners than either would have alone. And a rela-

tionship enjoying spiritual and emotional abundance is more likely
to survive and thrive.

A Rosmerta Candle Blessing: This spell can be cast in a variety of situations. If you are blessed with a stable, happy partnership, you
may simply wish to ask Rosmerta's blessings on your union. If your
partnership is less than ideal, Rosmerta may help you see how to
make it better. If you want a partner but don't have one, Rosmerta's
spell can help you open your inner energies to the possibility of
attracting someone new.

By the way, although the divine partnerships of old used male-
female imagery to symbolize fertility, there's no reason why this spell
won't work for those who prefer partners of the same sex. If choice
or circumstance leads you to build a life without a partner, you may
be interested in writing your own ritual to honor Rosmerta, asking
her to bless you with happy independence.

Place a red candle and a gold one in candleholders on your altar.
If you have a partner, decorate your ritual space with reminders of
this relationship—pictures of the two of you together, gifts you have
exchanged, clothing, or other personal items. If your partner is willing, he or she may participate in this ritual. Together, the two of you
should decide what blessings you will ask for as part of this ritual.

If you're doing this ritual alone, place on the altar symbols that
indicate to you some of the essential qualities you seek in your current or next partnership, or in yourself. Focus on the most important things—thoughtfulness rather than cooking skills, for example.
You might even write these qualities on a piece of paper and place
that on the altar. Also place on the altar a symbol of prosperity, perhaps a bowl of fruit or a handful of coins.

Once your circle has been cast, stand before the altar and close
your eyes. Clear your mind. If your partner is with you, hold hands.
This time, you'll invoke the goddess not through a direct call, but by
summoning up powerful imagery of her presence in your life.
Aloud, taking turns if you're with a partner, recite the blessings of
prosperity and love.

Prosperity is not about winning millions. Instead, it's that level of comfort which lets you take your mind off mere survival, so that you can focus at least a little of your time on learning, growth, and worship. You may not have much in the material world, but you can still call forth those things that give you a feeling of stability and abundance: solid friendships, access to a good library, healthy hands or eyes, connection to a community.

Speak these things. "I am blessed with a warm house." "We are blessed with the love of our friends." Let the feeling of abundance build as you talk of the natural riches of the place where you live, the possessions you treasure most, and the people who are closest to you. If you have a partner, speak of his or her best qualities, the ones that make you feel loved and treasured.

As this feeling of abundance grows, visualize your circle filling with soft golden light. When this light is bright in your mind, open your eyes and greet the goddess:

> *Hail, Rosmerta!*
> *Thou who art present*
> *In the words of love*
> *Thou who art present*
> *In the bounty of life*
> *Be welcome in this circle.*

Light the red candle. If two of you are doing this, light the candle together, two separate matches combining to create one flame. In your own words, ask the goddess for the blessings of a stable partnership. If you're in a very happy stage, this may end up being a description of the blessings you already enjoy, a rite of thanksgiving and devotion.

If you seek to improve an existing relationship, ask for the blessings that will help *you* be a better person within that relationship, rather than seeking to change your partner. Ask Rosmerta for insight or patience, for example, or for the strength to take care of yourself, or the wisdom to control your temper.

If your partner is present, listen carefully when he or she speaks. Put your whole focus on your partner's words, hearing them fully, without interrupting or judging, trying not to react emotionally. Improving a relationship doesn't mean there's anything wrong with you as a person; it's simply that all partners need to learn a great deal and work hard to stay together.

If you are without a partner, ask Rosmerta to help your inner self be open to the possibility of a new relationship. Don't be too specific about the details of your visualized partner—after all, you don't want to magically close the door to someone who might turn out to be a wonderful blessing. Instead, describe the things you'd enjoy doing with a partner, the vision that energizes you most about the idea of a lasting love. Ask Rosmerta to help you in the efforts you make to present yourself to potential partners as an attractive person.

Then offer your thanks, and say these words:

> *O Rosmerta,*
> *Thou who art present in the words of love*
> *Hear my words, receive my love*
> *Accept my thanks, and grant me thy wisdom*
> *That I may be worthy, that I may act wisely*
> *That I may be blessed with lasting love.*

Light the gold candle, and turn your attention now to Rosmerta as the goddess of prosperity and abundance. This time, choose just one blessing, a change of circumstance that would make a difference to your ability to learn and grow. Maybe you need to remove a source of strain by getting a bill paid. Perhaps a new job is necessary, or a new roommate. Whatever that one thing is, want it with all your being, then ask Rosmerta to bring it to you.

> *O Rosmerta,*
> *Thou who art present in the bounty of life*
> *I thank thee and honor thee*
> *For I am many times blessed.*
> *This thing I do ask*

That I may learn and grow.
If wisdom I do gain,
I dedicate it to thee.

Remain in meditation for a few minutes before the two candles, red and gold. You may be inspired during this time with ideas, wisdom, or energy to improve the abundance of love and wealth in your life. These inspirations are the gifts of Rosmerta.

Thank the goddess and end the rite according to your custom. Keep the candles together, perhaps wrapped in a green cloth, and burn them together when you have need of Rosmerta's emotional and material blessings.

Rosmerta in Daily Life: Rosmerta's blessings are those of stability. She is not the most exciting form of love goddess, but a necessary one. Stability is what allows children the best chance of growing up healthy and capable. Stability allows adults to spend time in learning and worship. Rosmerta's prosperity gives us room to spend time creating families, communities, and institutions that will sustain our descendants. Invoke her blessings on new enterprises and on marriages. Manifest her values by giving your time and skill to help prepare people for stable lives.

Give also your listening ear and practical assistance to those who are trying to form and sustain partnerships, for community support is one factor in the success of a marriage. Offer a night of babysitting so a couple can spend time alone, or make sure a new couple has a chance to spend time with others who offer living examples of strong, lasting love. Let teenagers know that their loves, too, are part of your community, and encourage them to form healthy, supportive relationships.

Sucellos

In History: Like Cernunnos, Sucellos (probably pronounced "Soo-KELL-os") is a convenient name applied to one type of god, in this case a hammer-god. In many places the spirit of the hammer-god was so strong that artisans used only the hammer symbol to indicate his presence.

Sucellos is often depicted alone, but is sometimes shown with his partner Nantosuelta, a goddess of the household whose icon was a small house on a tall pole. He is usually portrayed as a man of mature years, with curly hair and a beard, usually dressed in the clothing of a peasant. Often, he is shown with a vessel or barrel, indicative of his association with winemaking.

Sucellos, with or without his consort, is a god of fertility, healing, and fruitfulness. His are the bounties of the earth, and he was particularly popular in wine-making areas. Of the many depictions of this god, only one shows him as tipsy. This normally sober wine-god is quite a different being from the ecstatic Dionysus and Bacchus of the classical world.

Sucellos is a god of the harvest, of fertility in general, and especially with the fruitfulness of grapes used to make wine. Ancient wines were stronger and often sweeter than the ones we consider "good" now; they were transported at full strength, and diluted with water to suit the drinker's taste, or used to season food. Roman writers described the Celts' taste for alcoholic beverages as immoderate, though drunkenness was scarcely confined to any one segment of the ancient world.

Interestingly, scholars are not quite sure what the hammer is for. It may indicate thunder, or may be a symbol of industry. In many instances, it looks more like a mallet than a hammer, perhaps suggesting an implement used in sealing wine barrels. At least one writer, Miranda Green, is inclined to give it a more otherworldly interpretation, theorizing that the hammer indicated the awakening of life after winter or even life after death. Wisely, she notes that the Celts loved ambiguity, and that Sucellos' emblem—so powerful that it could stand alone as a depiction of this god's power—probably had many meanings.

In Modern Worship: Sucellos is one Celtic deity whose name has not been widely invoked in modern circles. In part, this is because many of his attributes are similar to those of better-known gods such as Cernunnos and Jupiter. Some writers have equated Sucellos with the club-wielding Irish gods Dagda and Ogma, mentioned in later texts. I am no scholar, but am inclined to disagree; Dagda seems a much cruder figure than the dignified portrayals of the ancient hammer-god, and a club is not a hammer.

Sucellos' role as a wine-god makes his worship a thought-provoking pursuit in this era of moderation. In the 1940s, Gerald Gardner recognized wine as one way of achieving "ways to the centre," that is, paths to the inner realms of the spirit, but cautioned that it may have bad aftereffects or be addictive. I prefer to achieve my magical contacts while in full control of my senses, and usually my chalice contains fruit juice. In worshiping Sucellos, I prefer to take his symbol of wine not with its literal meaning, but as a symbol of the altered state of consciousness one experiences in connecting with a god.

A Sucellos Spell: This is a spell for those moments when your fate rests in the hands of another. Perhaps you await the outcome of a court case, or a boss's decision on whether or not to hire you. Or perhaps your beloved is considering your marriage proposal, or you're hoping to get into a good school. This spell assumes you've done all you can in the outer world to show yourself worthy of the reward you seek.

Because you're going to be using a hammer during this ritual, you may need to do it outside your normal place. The silent circle casting here may prove useful to you in other circumstances where you cannot gather ritual items or prepare a space.

You'll need a hammer, three nails, a block of wood, a pencil, and perhaps a marker. You'll also need a cup of "wine"; as I mentioned above, fruit juice is fine. (For an authentic touch, look for fruits known to the ancient Celts, such as strawberries, raspberries, cherries, or blackberries.) Once you've assembled these items, find a time and space where you can be alone. Be aware that you're going to be making noise, and choose your setting with respect for others' sensibilities.

Stand facing the north, if you can. (If you don't already do this, it's a good idea to start becoming aware of which direction you are facing at all times.) Close your eyes and breathe deeply as you ground and center.

With your eyes still closed, visualize a circle of gentle green light around the perimeter of a circle with you at the center. This is the soft glow that pervades places of nature such as forests, arbors, or fields full of crops. Breathe deeply as you clear your mind of all sights except this one.

Once the visualization is solidly in your mind, continue to take deep breaths, and each time you exhale, see the circle's light grow a little brighter. As the light increases, you begin to see that the circle is surrounded by tall vine-covered trees that form a barrier between you and the outside world. Remain where you are, eyes shut and breathing deeply, until this green barrier is firmly embedded in your consciousness. Then, when you are ready, open your eyes and begin the spell.

Take up the hammer in your dominant hand, and hold it upright. Aloud or in your mind, invoke the god:

> *Sucellos, whose every blow strikes true*
> *God of the vine and field and tree*
> *I offer my sacrifice to you*
> *And pray that your blessings be granted to me*
> *Sucellos, guide my hand!*

Put down the hammer and settle down with your pencil and block of wood. Take a few moments to meditate upon your desired outcome, visualizing yourself enjoying its benefits and using them to learn and grow as a person. Then, dwelling upon this visualization, draw a simple symbol on the wood that will indicate (at least to you) the outcome you seek.

If you can't think of anything to draw, let your mind drift back to the visualization for a few moments to allow the god to inspire you. Draw carefully, but do not worry too much about making the image perfect—it's far more important to put your own concentration and creative energy into it.

When you are done drawing your image, take up the hammer and one of your nails as you focus once more on your goal.

Sucellos, ancient god
Guide my hand in this work of magic
As I will it, so shall it be
This, or something better!

Carefully but firmly hammer the nail into a point on your image. As you hammer, see yourself sealing the desired outcome in place. Repeat the words as you hammer in the other two nails.

Now take up the "wine," and drink a toast to Sucellos, offering him your worship and thanks. If you are outdoors, pour out the rest of the liquid onto the earth. Otherwise, offer it to the earth as soon as you can after the spell is done.

Finally, close your eyes and breathe deeply, returning your focus to the green wall of vine-covered trees that has protected your sacred space. Focus also on the ring of light that defines the space in your mind. With each breath, see the light of the circle grow a little dimmer, until the greenery has faded from view, and still dimmer until the space is dark once more.

Keep the block of wood in your ritual space or with your sacred objects until the fateful moment has passed. You may wish to use it again for similar rites, dedicating it to Sucellos and inscribing it with symbols of your faith and progress.

Sucellos in Daily Life: Sucellos watches over all aspects of fertility. Connect to his energy by growing green things, buying produce from local farms and vineyards, and working to help preserve farmland in your area. Pray to him when trying to conceive a baby, and honor him by making responsible decisions about your own reproductive health.

Many Wiccans and Pagans enjoy making their own mead, beer, or wine, often using local honey, grain, or fruit, and celebrating the fact that each bottle is unique. Sucellos' true essence is not invoked by getting drunk, but by using the fruits of the earth in moderation and without loss of dignity.

Coventina

In History: Coventina was a local goddess, worshiped at one place in northern England. Because that place—Coventina's Well, in what is now Carrawburgh, Northumbria—has been excavated and its artifacts preserved, we can develop some ideas about how she was worshiped, and learn a great deal about her essence.

As the presiding deity of a well, she is representative of the many goddesses who governed bodies of water. Wells and springs were sacred not only because they provided essential water, but also as places of offering to the gods.

Coventina's Well was most popular during the Roman period, but that doesn't mean the people who worshiped there came from Rome. The empire drew heavily on conquered Celtic peoples for troops to maintain its borders, and Celtic and Germanic names are found on the altars set up to honor Coventina. (Possibly because of the travels of soldiers and officials, a couple of altars to Coventina have been found in Spain and France, hundreds of miles from her sacred well.) Also in the well were thousands of coins, plus bronze statues, glass and ceramic vessels, jewelry, a human skull, and more than twenty stone altars.

Some of this material was offered by worshipers to Coventina. Some of it may have been placed there for safekeeping during a time when the area was threatened, or in response to the Roman emperor Theodosius' edict of 391 C.E., which closed all Pagan temples and banned all forms of non-Christian worship. Some of it may have been discarded, the well used as a trash receptacle by those who didn't like or didn't care about the goddess.

It's reasonable to say that many people *did* worship Coventina and leave offerings in the well as a way of asking her favor or offering her devotion. Some of the offered items were deliberately broken or otherwise rendered useless before being deposited, which was typical in Celtic sacrifices. This tends to indicate that the item itself wasn't the important part of the sacrifice—what counted was giving up the use of it.

Scholars think the well was bounded by a rectangular stone wall, but was open to the sky. Perhaps the best-known altar depicts Coventina as a water nymph, naked from the waist up and reclining gracefully on the bank of a stream (or, perhaps, on a leaf), holding a water lily in her right hand.

Many of the altars from Coventina's Well offer thanks to the goddess for favors conferred upon the donor. This was a common practice of the Roman era imported into Celtic territory. Those who had reason to be grateful to a god or goddess would pay a craftsman to build a stone altar, anywhere from a few inches to several feet high. The stone would be inscribed on the sides, with a flat surface on the top for offering incense or wine, and the giver would have it installed in the temple to be seen by all.

Lindsay Allason-Jones and Bruce MacKay, scholars who created a comprehensive account of the items found in the well, note that Coventina appears to have been an "all-rounder," that is, a goddess whose power was not associated with any one aspect of life, but whose blessings might be sought for any purpose. The evidence of the well does not indicate that its waters had any special healing power ascribed to them, though no doubt healing was one of the blessings people sought from the goddess. Offerings to Coventina appear to have been made in attitudes of gratitude or hopeful prayer, rather than propitiating a fearsome power.

In Modern Worship: Some modern Wiccans have made the trip to Northumbria to find Coventina's Well. The area is rich with history and beauty, and the trip is a worthwhile one for those who can make it. I have done this twice, and both times found evidence that modern Pagan worshipers were holding rites at the nearby Temple of Mithras. On our honeymoon, my husband and I traveled to the site, which was too wet to explore directly. Instead, we chose a secluded hill overlooking the Well, made an offering of incense and asked her blessing on our partnership.

It's fair to say, though, that you're not going to make it to the north of England every time you want to call on Coventina. It's perfectly reasonable to choose some spring, well, stream, or pond near your own home and use it as a point of contact with this goddess. Indoors, you might try a tabletop fountain or vessel of water.

Because her name contains the word "coven," a few Wiccans have connected Coventina with the work of forming, protecting, and sustaining Wiccan groups. There's no evidence that the two words have any sort of relationship, and such a connection should be regarded as imaginative rather than historical. Though many theories have been advanced, no one knows what Coventina's name means or where it came from. Like the goddess herself, the name is both beautiful and mysterious.

A Coventina Spell: This is one of the simplest types of spell, and one that has the strongest roots in the Celtic past.

Find a body of water that has meaning to you. Ideally, this will be a small pond or spring, but any water will do—lake, ocean, or brook. This may require taking some time to explore the places of nature near your home, which will help you gain knowledge of the spirit of the place where you live. In my previous house, I was lucky enough to be able to walk to a waterfall, which was particularly effective as a ritual spot.

Visit your special place at a time when you can have at least a little time and space to yourself. Take time to explore the place, enjoying the beauty of the water and familiarizing yourself with the natural life that surrounds it.

Become still, and gaze upon the water, opening your inner self to any thoughts or images that it might inspire. Then, when you are ready, take the largest-denomination coin you have and hold it in your dominant hand.

> *To the goddess Coventina*
> *And the spirit of this place*
> *I make this gift*
> *In thanks for my blessings*
> *And in token of my devotion*

Offer a prayer for some personal concern, or simply assure Coventina of your worship. Return to this place and renew the offering once a season.

As part of this ritual, take care of the place. Pick up litter (and, of course, leave no trash behind). If the area is a public place used by crowds, keep to established trails to protect the vegetation. Each time you visit, be truly aware of the place, and of the changes that the months and years have wrought.

Coventina in Daily Life: The essence of this goddess is strongly related to water, which is essential to all life. Today, with widespread convenient plumbing, we tend to take water for granted. Understanding and appreciating water can help you become more attuned to Coventina's energy.

Learn the source of the water you drink, and what happens to it after it goes down your drain. Take action in your community to safeguard your sources of water and ensure the safest possible disposal of wastewater. In your own home, avoid wasting water. Health experts say many of us don't drink enough water. Try substituting plain water for at least one of the sodas, juices, or cups of coffee you might otherwise drink during the day.

Cerridwen

In History: While this goddess is widely known as a Celtic deity, there is no evidence of her whatsoever before about the ninth century, when apparently her name was first given to the sorceress in a Welsh poet's story. In this tale, Cerridwen (pronounced "ker-RID-wen") brews a magical potion intended to give the gift of inspiration to her child. Instead, her servant accidentally swallows the concoction. She chases the servant through a variety of shape-changes, until finally she swallows him and gives birth to him again in the form of the revered poet Taliesin.

Cerridwen's name means "crooked woman," and she appears in this literature as a stereotypical "witch"—unattractive, selfish, and endowed with magical knowledge. The elements of her tale—shape-shifting, a magical vessel, a potion gone astray—are common to folk tales from many cultures. But in Welsh literature, Cerridwen was associated firmly with the cauldron of inspiration from that time forward. Other Welsh poets of the period took up her story, and wrote of her as the source of their own inspiration. Through this poetic tribute came the perception of Cerridwen as a goddess, which continues to this day.

In Modern Worship: If Cerridwen wasn't a goddess of the Pagan Celts, why include her in a book about Celtic Wicca? Because the early Wiccans, coming across the name of this supposedly ancient goddess, added her to their pantheon. A great many Wiccans have worshiped the historically unrelated Cerridwen and Cernunnos as a divine couple, perhaps because their names sounded good together. In this pairing, she is usually seen as a universal goddess of inspiration. Others, more familiar with her tale, associate Cerridwen with the archetype of the "dark goddess," who governs our destructive capabilities and our hidden selves.

It is a guiding principle of Wicca that people directing their spiritual energy toward an object or an idea can transform it. If you have performed or attended Wiccan rituals, you have probably already seen this: By using various magical techniques and concentrating on their goal, Wiccans can transform a living room or a backyard into a magical temple, a place of power. Thus it is with a magical name. Cerridwen, worshiped by thousands, is real to those who have called her name in prayer and devotion. Even a newcomer will find her essence relatively easy to invoke because of this built-up energy.

(Many Wiccans deliberately set out to evoke a similar effect in themselves by taking another name when they are initiated. By doing this, they seek to build spiritual energy around a name and identity that has been chosen by themselves, rather than bestowed by others. Such a name also has some protective effects if you don't feel comfortable letting others connect your real identity with a faith that still has many misconceptions to overcome.)

If your goal is to get as close as possible to the ancient worship of the Celts, you may wish to concentrate your energies on other deities. On the other hand, if you find her story compelling, or if perhaps you join a group that invokes Cerridwen regularly, by all means worship her, for her power is real.

A Spell of Cerridwen: The story tells how Cerridwen gathered herbs and boiled them for a year and a day to make the magical potion. It was meant to give her son a gift to establish him in the society of that time, which might have been inclined to hate him because of his ugliness. (Beauty isn't everything. A later tale describes this same son emerging unhurt from a battle because he was so ugly that everyone thought he was a demon.)

This spell involves not a potion, but a ritual bath, using herbs to purify oneself and as an aid to meditation. Cast this spell when you've been subjected to a lot of chaotic or negative influences, when you want to prepare for an initiation or other important ritual, or when you want to heal your own body image.

If you're not experienced with herbs, do not try to gather them in the wild. This caution is more important when choosing herbs for internal use, for you can do yourself serious physical harm by taking the wrong one, or by failing to properly understand both your symptoms and the herb's effects. If you're sure you know what you're doing, or can consult a trained expert, harvest your leaves or flowers with consideration. Refrain from taking all plants of a given species from a given area, and leave an offering (perhaps some bird-seed) in the place where you gather.

An ideal way to make sure you're getting the herbs you want is to grow them yourself. Even then, be careful about labeling both the plants and any herbal concoctions you make. Failing that, seek out a reliable herb store, preferably one where the staff is knowledgeable and willing to spend time sharing information.

There are several books that list the ritual purposes of various herbs. Remember that your own experiences and sensations are the best guide. I'll offer three suggestions for this rite; choose the one that you find most suitable.

Lavender is a powerful and pleasant herb for purification. In addition, its energy helps protect and purify a room or home.

Honeysuckle was known to the Welsh poets of old, and is useful for stability and renewal.

Lovage is a less well-known herb that herbalist Paul Beyerl describes as being powerful in drawing romance, especially when the practitioner is male.

Whatever your chosen herb, you don't need a great deal of it for your bath—a handful of fresh or dried leaves, or a few drops of the essential oil. If using leaves, place them in a cheesecloth bag (sold in herb stores). For a truly luxurious experience that will leave your skin feeling great, add four tablespoons of honey and a quarter-cup of mineral oil to the bath water. Enhance your bathing experience, if you like, by lighting the bathroom with candles and arranging soft, meditative music.

Cast a sacred circle in your bathing space, then run a bath at a comfortable temperature and add the items you have prepared. While the water is running, invoke Cerridwen's presence:

> *Cerridwen, Cerridwen, Cauldron Queen*
> *Wash away worry and leave me clean*
> *Help me to understand what I see*
> *Help me to know of thy mystery*

Enter the bath. Use your hands or feet to stir the water. Relax in the water, feeling your skin absorb the cleansing energy. Feel the water surrounding you—not like ordinary water, but like a foundation surrounds the bottom of a statue.

Physically cleanse yourself—not with soap, but with the water that surrounds you, using your own hands as well as any cloth or brush you may normally employ. (If you put honey in the water, you may wish to either keep your hair dry or rinse it afterward.) Wash your body in long strokes, metaphorically sweeping away stress, worry, anger, or whatever is "polluting" to you. Take time to admire your body, finding its beauties and strengths and consciously washing away negative perceptions.

Remain in meditation in the bath, feeling yourself cleansed and immersed in the Cauldron of Inspiration. If there is a question facing you, speak it in a whisper, then clear your mind and allow the goddess to offer you an answer.

When you are ready to leave the bath, stand, turning off the water and opening the drain. As the water spirals down the drain, visualize all the impurities you have washed away go spiraling downward. When all the water is gone, dry yourself and step out of the bath. Bid Cerridwen a respectful farewell, and end the rite according to your custom.

If you do not have a bathtub in your living space, you may be able to adapt this ritual by using a potpourri pot, with a votive candle underneath, to help disseminate the scent of your chosen herb through your shower area.

In Daily Life: Honor Cerridwen by making the most of your creativity, whatever forms it may take. Honor her also by giving thanks to the people and gods who inspire you to persevere.

Cerridwen's energy is also found among those who learn about the plants of the earth and the ways they can be used to enhance both spirit and body. Many Wiccans enjoy making their own incense, scented oils, or even soap. Besides providing a pleasant pastime, this is an interesting way to gain personal experience of various scents and energies and their magical properties. Growing an herb garden helps foster a connection with nature and a deep understanding of the earth where you live.

Others study the paths of healing, often with a special view to the ways nature provides all that we need. While all of us have healing abilities, using them wisely requires concentration, book learning, and maturity. Whether you're a surgeon or a massage therapist, you will be most effective at helping others when you study with more experienced people, act only within the limits of your training and understand the person behind the problem.

As I mentioned at the beginning of this chapter, these are only a few of the many deities known to Celtic Wiccan practitioners. I encourage you to look up these goddesses and gods for yourself, and to find others whose stories or imagery you may find compelling.

Most likely, you will end up with a small group of gods and goddesses with whom you feel a strong connection. Some people feel such a strong connection to one deity in particular that they claim that god or goddess is their "patron" or "matron." Such a relationship can last a lifetime, but it is not necessary to have one patron deity, nor is it impossible to change deities from time to time, adopting new ones into your personal pantheon while continuing to respect those whose energies are no longer as necessary in your life.

The rituals in this chapter provide a sampling of some basic magical and meditative workings. While they are perfectly functional rites, they will work best for you if you consider them as templates rather than as set-in-stone liturgy. Read through each ritual a couple of times to understand its intent, then adapt it in whatever way will make it most meaningful for you. Your creativity can help make the difference between a simple devotion and a deep, meaningful experience.

FOUR

Constructing a Celtic Wiccan Ritual

By now, you've seen a number of spells and rituals, and I hope you've tried a few. You probably found that some were more effective for you than others, and you may be starting to get a feel for your own magical personality, for what practices and pursuits help you to feel closest to the divine.

Wicca is a religion of individuals, incorporating the belief that each person can learn enough to function as his or her own priest or priestess. This is different from many mainstream religions, which tend to follow standard liturgies and establish groups of trained practitioners (priests, ministers, or rabbis) to perform them. Many Wiccans write their own rituals, either as part of a personal practice or as part of group training and leadership. Crafting a ritual is interesting, challenging, and sometimes difficult work.

There are many ways of writing and enacting a ritual. You can, for example, adapt any of the rituals in this book to suit your needs.

You can also "wing it" and make them up on the spot. Even simple acts, such as drinking a toast to the full moon or letting the summer sun wash over your body, can become rituals if you perform them with worshipful or magical intent.

Here, however, I will outline a more complex process, aimed at giving the practitioner the closest possible alignment of mind and spirit with a chosen god or goddess of ancient times. This process is based on techniques used by Western magical groups for decades. In following it, my goal is to balance historical facts, the divine guidance of the goddess or god, and my own judgment of what is appropriate and important in the here and now.

This process can and should be adapted to your own intentions and circumstances. The more you read and learn and create, and the more work you do to grow as a Wiccan and as a human being, the better equipped you will be to create rituals that are truly inspired and truly your own.

Is all of this preparation necessary? Yes and no. When the need arises, Wiccans can create perfectly effective rituals from the materials at hand, relying on the knowledge and experience they already have. When a pair of students wanted to do a project on Wicca, they watched as three other Wiccans and I spent ninety minutes planning a ritual, then performed it with and for the documentary team. When I was in severe back pain one day and couldn't bend down, I improvised a healing ritual for myself using only items that were on the middle or upper shelves of one room. Yet thorough preparation helps lay the groundwork for such spontaneous experiences by adding to your store of learning.

Purpose

Before you begin to record your thoughts and ideas, make some specific decisions about the event and its purpose. You may start with a simple idea: "I want to have a bonfire ritual and invite a bunch of Wiccan friends over." If you don't refine and clarify this idea, the result will probably be a decent party, but a failure as a spiritual experience. Likewise, if you have several things going on at once—say, a prosperity ritual plus someone's naming ceremony plus blessing someone's home—it will be difficult for you to raise and focus enough energy for each goal.

Each ritual has a different purpose, of course, but most Wiccan rituals can be grouped into one of three areas:

Worship and Celebration. These are vital and important elements, and it is quite normal to devote a rite solely to these purposes. Worship rites help the practitioner build a connection to a god or goddess through acts and words of devotion, and through meditation on the divine presence. Such rituals also build up the influence of that deity by directing the participants' energy toward honoring the goddess or god.

Celebration rites are joyous expressions recognizing and appreciating the ancient deities' influence in our lives. If done by more than one person, they also affirm the practitioners' bonds to one another in "perfect love and perfect trust," traditional Wiccan words that define the peace and friendship necessary to perform spiritual work together. They are frequently performed at the eight Wiccan holidays (see the chapter on Seasonal Rituals).

Worship and celebration rituals are the simplest rites, and the ones most suitable for a public setting. They often provide the best introduction for those who are new to ritual, and are most likely to engage the energy of a large and diverse group.

At some Pagan and Wiccan festivals, such rituals are performed to honor "the Goddess," "the God," or both, as a way of including the wide range of deities honored by the many people attending. While this is understandable in a large-group situation, the Celts would not have envisioned their pantheon in this way, believing instead in individual divine beings with their own very distinct attributes. In my own practice, I have found that aligning one's mind and spirit with a specific deity is far more powerful than generic worship of all divinity.

When practical, worship rituals often allow each participant a personal moment of communion with the deity or a chance to express a personal goal or concern. This helps keep newcomers or members of a large group from feeling "lost in the crowd."

These rituals often include universal aspects of celebration, such as sharing a meal, singing, dancing, chanting, or telling jokes or stories.

Learning, Growth, and Magic. In this category are all the rituals designed to have an effect on a person or situation in the world beyond the circle. Most spellwork falls into this category, even if the purpose is related to the practitioner's religious life, for learning and growing spiritually makes you a better person in all aspects of your being. Such rituals may be very personal: for example, a solitary practitioner seeking to get a better job or become more attractive to a new lover. They may be based in the community: for example, a group raising healing energy for a member's difficult pregnancy. Or such rituals may be done to raise energy toward goals that go far beyond the Wiccan world, such as environmental healing or freedom of religion.

These rituals can help foster each participant's own spiritual growth. They are also well suited for groups of people who worship together regularly, or who have gathered around a single cause. When preparing for such a ritual, it is important that everyone be aware of the purpose, and in agreement with it, before the rite begins. (This may sound obvious, but there have been cases where the leaders got halfway through the ritual before revealing that its purpose was to further some political cause that some of the participants did not support.)

Initiations. These rites, whether performed by a group or by an individual, recognize and test a person's spiritual progress, allowing elder practitioners and the gods and goddesses to confer acknowledgments of that progress. These are often the most formal and complex rites, and they should not be performed without a great deal of thought and planning. Their effects are lifelong.

In Wicca, there are traditionally three "degrees" of initiation, a concept borrowed from Freemasonry. Different groups have different systems for granting such degrees, but generally they look something like this:

First Degree Initiate: Has studied the beliefs and practices of the religion and is capable of conducting personal rituals.

Second Degree Initiate: Has undertaken further learning and is capable of leading a group in study or worship.

Third Degree Initiate: Has many years of experience in ritual, spellwork, and teaching, and is acclaimed as a leader.

This category also includes rituals intended to mark life-changing events. Examples include the welcoming of a new baby, the passage of a child into physical maturity, marriage (called "handfasting" by Wiccans), divorce ("handparting"), the passage into old age ("croning" for women; no standard term for men has yet evolved), and the ritual of honoring someone who has died (sometimes called "requiem").

Once you have decided which category of ritual you seek to create, focus on the results you desire: What feelings do you want the participants to have during the ritual? What magic will be accomplished? What actions would you like people to take as a result of having taken part in this ritual? Write down your answers to these questions, and refine your original statement.

For instance, "I want to do a bonfire ritual and invite a bunch of Wiccan friends over" might evolve through thought and planning into "This ritual will celebrate the god Cernunnos and the essence of the winter season." Or it could become "This ritual will be a solemn experience of sacred power, bringing us together to ask the goddess Brigid whether we should form a coven." (This assumes the group agrees it's a good question to ask.)

Back to the Books

Now that you've decided why you're doing this ritual, it's important to learn more about the deities you wish to invoke. Because Celtic Wicca has history as its foundation, you'll want to make sure you invoke gods and goddesses whose history is most in tune with the intention of your rite. Even if you regularly invoke the same god, goddess, or divine couple, this phase of ritual-writing offers a good time to return to your books and focus on what is known from history, with a special eye to your current purpose.

If you're like me, and love books, this is a fun phase of ritual construction. Get hold of all the information you can. (See the bibliography for some suggestions for investigating the vast wealth of information that's available.)

If you can afford to buy books, it's a worthwhile endeavor to build a Celtic library bit by bit. That way, you don't have to worry about not having information because it's out of print, someone stole it from the library or you suddenly developed a need to check a fact in the middle of the night. Also, by buying books about Celtic history and Wiccan religion, you help encourage the publication of more books with those themes.

But you needn't go without useful information because of lack of funds. If you use it, a library card can provide one of the cheapest forms of education available. Get to your local college library (most of them will allow members of the community access to their collections for a small fee), or to a large public library. In the United States, a program called Interlibrary Loan can help you borrow books from libraries many miles away.

Most Wiccans adore books, but those who seek to honor the ancient gods of Britain have a particular need to read many sources of information and evaluate them carefully. You will often find that different writers interpret the same piece of information in many different ways. By reading you will begin to develop a sense of which sources offer the best reasoning—not the ones whose ideas are most appealing, but the ones whose work makes the most sense and is best supported by facts. Be wary of books by people who say they have all the answers.

If you don't have a deity in mind, but have a theme you wish to express, your investigations will focus on the way the ancient Celts dealt with similar ideas, and which gods they associated with those ideas. Also, any writings or artwork after about the year 400 will be affected by the spread of Christianity. You may still be able to get good information on Pagan religion from works created after that time, but it's important to acknowledge the strong influence of the newer religion.

Wherever possible, get visual information as well as written words, for the Celts' art is their most direct communication with us. Make note of the ancient associations of a particular deity—animals, natural places, times of year, clothing, symbolic items. Consult the works of historians to gain an understanding of the probable meaning of those associations. Where their ideas conflict (and they will), look at the available factual evidence and use your own best judgment.

Researching a Deity: Sulis

Let's assume that you and I want to write a worship ritual to Sulis, the powerful healing goddess of the hot-water spring in what is now Bath, England. We might be able to draw on actual experiences of Aquae Sulis, the Roman Baths where she was honored of old. If we haven't been there, books and photographs can give us significant information about her sacred site.

Even if we've read a lot about Sulis before, it will help us go back to our books and read again, this time with a view toward writing the planned worship ritual. Here's a synopsis of what we might discover:

Sulis was the patron goddess of a hot spring, and both the goddess and the waters were believed to have had healing and magical powers. Because of this, the Romans associated her with their Minerva, also a goddess of healing. She was the only female Celtic deity given such a double name, though Mars and Jupiter were given surnames representing a variety of local gods. Sulis Minerva's name is unique in another way: The Celtic name comes first, perhaps indicating the power and popularity of her worship.

Archaeologist Barry Cunliffe notes that widespread Roman building, including an ambitious drainage system for the spring, probably destroyed most of whatever the pre-Roman population had left at the site. Cunliffe did discover the remains of a Celtic stone pathway leading up to the spring, with wooden stakes along the sides; he also found eighteen Celtic coins there.

Aquae Sulis, the Roman complex of altars, bathhouses, and courtyards, became a destination for the middle and upper classes of Romano-British society. Yet the presence of those few Celtic coins, as well as the prominence of her native name, indicate that this goddess's powers were honored well before the Roman conquest.

Among the significant items discovered at this site are a few large pieces of artwork. One is a bronze face representing the goddess, probably crafted during Roman times and portraying her in the guise of a serene, mysterious Minerva.

Another major religious piece connected with Sulis is a massive stone face that shows much more Celtic influence. It is male, with flowing hair and beard forming a sunlike circle, yet some of the strands of hair form the shapes of snakes or perhaps fish, reflecting the water imagery natural to such a place. This circular image formed the center of a triangular lintel, with helmets below decorated with an owl and a dolphin.

This does not appear to be the same deity as that depicted on the bronze face—or is it? Possibly Sulis had both male and female aspects, and androgynous deities are known in many parts of the world. Celtic societies tended to identify a focus of worship firmly as either god or goddess, but the use of ambiguity and symbolism was common in a more general sense. Or, possibly, the "Gorgon" is the representation of a consort of Sulis. Yet the many altars found in that place name no god, only Sulis Minerva, always identified in the inscriptions as Dea, or "goddess."

Further fascinating information about Sulis Minerva can be drawn from the thousands of items thrown into the sacred spring by those offering prayers to her. Many offered coins, while some offered small symbolic objects; Miranda Green notes in particular the offering of a pair of ivory breasts, and theorizes that they were a charm to heal or prevent the failure of a woman's milk.

Other worshipers inscribed their prayers on sheets of lead. These "curse tablets" date from the Roman period, but a few Celtic names can be found therein, among the pleas to Sulis for healing, for the return of stolen property, and in one notable case for the punishment of "he who carried off Vilbia from me," possibly seeking the goddess's help in revenge for luring a lover away.

Thus we see a powerful and complex deity, strongly associated with water, yet also with the sun. Sulis in history held the power to heal and to right wrongs, and was worshiped by a wide spectrum of society. Today her spring is part of a museum that draws thousands of tourists every year. Echoing the acts of their predecessors, they toss coins into a pool of hot spring water. Today, though, their cash does not stay in the earth, but goes to help with research and upkeep of the site.

A Divine Presence

Once you've accumulated facts to support the ritual you want to write, an excellent next step is to craft a "pre-ritual" or "meditation ritual." This is a simple guided meditation in which you use the information you've gathered to form an initial spiritual connection. By basing your ritual on what is known from history, you're reaching back to the Celtic faith of antiquity. By meditating with this information as a focus, you allow the god or goddess an opportunity to help you craft the ritual, to reveal to you directly what worship is most suitable.

Use your research to construct a mental image of a temple, shrine, or natural landscape that might have been associated with this deity in history. This mental image might be termed an "inner temple," and the pre-ritual will consist of a meditation in which you go on a journey to that temple and invoke the deity within it. The "outer temple"—your ritual space in the physical world—should correspond in some small way to this mental image.

Write down an outline of your meditation, or record it onto a tape to play back to yourself during the ritual. Once you've done it a couple of times, you should have the imagery fairly well committed to memory.

As you do the meditation, you may find it helps fix the journey in your mind if you speak the steps, aloud or in a whisper, as you move through them. If you're going to guide a group in this meditation later on, it is especially important for you to practice saying the words, so that you get an idea of the right pacing. Your listeners need time not only to hear your words, but also to understand them and reflect on the inner experiences those words evoke.

Meditation: Sulis

Now that we've read whatever information we can find, trying to draw careful conclusions from the facts, it's time to use the information to try to forge a spiritual connection to Sulis.

To prepare, we begin by crafting a simple invocation based on our research and our intent. In particular, we return to the books and reread Barry Cunliffe's brief passage imagining what the site of the spring might have looked like before the Romans arrived:

> *The springs emerged on a promontory of land, thrust out from the limestone upland of Lansdown, protected on three sides by the fast-flowing river . . . The river snaked across a wide flood plain . . . Marshy, braided with small streams and choked with vegetation, it would have formed a formidable barrier except to those who knew the more solid ground and the fords. . . .*
>
> *To see the hot steamy water gush out of the opening in the side of the Roman reservoir today is an awe-inspiring sight. How much more dramatic would the flow of water have been in the natural surroundings of 2,000 years ago, the vivid orange-red of the iron salts violent and unsettling against the natural greens and greys, the whole scene made more frightening by the uncertain movements of the hovering steam. Little wonder that the place was thought to belong to the gods. (Roman Bath, pp. 11–12)*

We will need to imagine some details of our own to make this a fully formed visualization, but the archaeologist's account helps us ground our imaginings in fact.

What are we going to do about the gender ambiguity suggested by that great, indubitably male Celtic face that appeared above the

Roman temple? It is difficult to ignore, but it may be distracting to try to address it directly in our ritual. Instead, let's decorate the altar with pictures of both the bronze "Minerva" and the stone "Gorgon." From force of habit, and without direct contradictory evidence, I will continue to visualize Sulis as a goddess. Nonetheless, we might try to purposely limit our gender references. With this approach we may be able to meditate on the essence of Sulis, allowing that essence to be revealed to us in whatever way our chosen deity sees fit.

When we get ready for the ritual, the altar will include both the deity images plus a photograph of the spring at Aquae Sulis. We might choose green and gold candles to tie in with the imagery of water in general, and the green-gold water of her spring in particular. To make ourselves comfortable, we'll place two armchairs opposite the altar, with a chalice of water on a central table and a notebook and pen nearby.

As we ground and center ourselves, we'll use the image of the spring as a visual focus, then cast a circle and call the quarters. Summoning up a sincere intention and desire for Sulis' presence, we stand before the altar, raise our arms and invoke her:

> *Warmth of the sun*
> *Mystery of the deep earth*
> *Power of the flowing water*
> *Sulis!*
>
> *Healing of ills*
> *Righting of wrongs*
> *Cleansing of impurity*
> *Sulis!*
>
> *Sight of the owl*
> *Hearing of the dolphin*
> *Speed of the snake*
> *Sulis!*

We remain there, eyes shut, until an inner sense tells us Sulis has entered our circle. (More on this later.)

Bowing to the altar to acknowledge Sulis' presence, we move to the chairs, relax for a moment and then begin the meditation. When two people are meditating together, try having one person describe a step of the journey in a low voice, then rap on a table or chair arm when done. Then the second person echoes that step, and raps to continue. The repetition has the effect of reinforcing the imagery while making sure you both end up in the same place.

You are standing in a place of shadows. Before you is a double door of ancient oak. You make a Sign of Entering, and the doors swing outward before you. You step out the door onto a gravel path that travels straight up a low green hill. Cool mist fills the air, yet you can make out a river in the distance ahead of you.

Around you lie swamps, watery ground filled with green growth and clumps of trees. You keep to the gravel path and stay on dry land. You approach the top of the hill, surrounded on three sides by the river, with a few gray stones showing through the green growth of the misty hillside.

You pause and listen for a moment, hearing far-off calls of birds—and, much closer, a bubbling flow of water. Moving toward this sound, you reach a compelling and mysterious sight: an orange-red opening in the gray stone, with water pouring forth. Though the air is cool, the water is hot, steam pouring forth from the opening in the earth and forming a green pool before flowing downhill toward the river. The spring smells like fire and stone combined, sharp yet not displeasing.

You breathe deeply of the moist air of the spring, and offer a prayer to the divine ruler of this sacred place. Before your eyes the mist begins to coalesce, and the image of Sulis forms above the pool, beautiful and grave, with compelling wide eyes and floating hair, draped in a flowing green cloak fastened with an elaborate gold pin.

At this point, with this visualization firmly established in our minds, we fall silent to interact with Sulis at the spring. In my visualization, I offer respectful greetings, then ask Sulis to show me how best to worship her. I then sit in silent meditation, awaiting any information Sulis might choose to share with us.

In my mind's eye, Sulis accepts my greetings graciously, and seems pleased that we have chosen to invoke her. Her image, distinctly female, never departs from the space above the spring, but her face and hands help convey her message.

Usually, the gods communicate with me through images, but in this case a sentence pops into my mind: "The spring is the sacred." Then I see an image of someone dipping two fingers into a golden bowl of water and dabbing it on hands, heart, and forehead.

All this time, of course, you've been in your own meditation, perhaps receiving very different information. Once again, if two or more people are meditating together, use the signal of rapping on the chair to indicate when each person is ready to move to the closing meditation. When both are ready, we begin the journey out:

> *Sulis indicates to you that she has no further communication to offer. You bow your head in respect, then look up to find the image has faded, the spring and pool surrounded once more only by swirling mist.*
>
> *You find that you have brought a coin in offering, a small bit of bronze decorated with a stylized depiction of a horse and rider. You offer a farewell, then drop the coin into the pool.*
>
> *Turning, you return to the gravel path, following it through the mist as the sound of the water fades. You descend the hill and return to the portal through which you entered. You step within the doors, and they swing shut behind you. You remain for a moment in the place of shadows, then return fully to this place and time.*

We stay seated with our eyes shut for a moment, taking in the sounds and smells of the room and grounding any excess energy inspired by the meditation.

At this point, we may wish to discuss our experiences with one another, or to write them down for later reference. Then we rise, taking up the chalice of water. We decide to follow the action I saw in meditation, dipping our fingers in the water and then touching palms, heart, and forehead. Then we lift the cup toward the altar as if making a toast, and address Sulis:

> Ruler of the sacred water,
> Essence of the holy spring,
> Of fire and earth you are the daughter.
> Accept our thanks and offering.
> Hail and farewell!

After this, we dismiss the quarters and close the circle, reversing the steps we took to create our sacred space.

While it is not usually necessary to perform a grounding meditation after such a quiet ritual, it is helpful to do something physical. Having something to eat—even just a few crackers or a little fruit— works well. If we haven't already written down what we saw during the meditation, we should do so now, so that we may refer to this information in planning the final ritual.

Now, you may believe that the goddess Sulis appeared before us and spoke to us. Or you may believe that the words and images that came to us were suggested by our own subconscious minds, helped by our research and the familiar actions of setting up a circle and invoking a deity. If you ask me which is correct, I will say "both," and mean it. I believe that the gods of my worship are the creators and sustainers of all life, including mine. If the information I supposedly get from the gods comes from my own mind, who but the gods gave me that mind and the opportunity to use it? I do not know how this process works; I do know that it does work.

Of course, this same format may be used for much more than ritual planning. You might do this meditation to seek Sulis' influence in your life, perhaps to gain her guidance in deciding how best to heal yourself or someone else, or whether to take action against a wrongdoer.

For many groups, or for a public circle, a meditation ritual requires more mental discipline and calls up far more complex imagery than is necessary or practical. The exception might be a small coven or meditation circle that meets regularly, forming a stable core of people focused on such work.

For the persons leading a ritual, these meditations are a valuable form of preparation. When preparing to offer a ritual to a group of people, I try to do a meditation like this at least once, and preferably three times, in the preceding month.

How Do You Know It's Working?

You've invoked a god or goddess: Now what?

This is one of the parts of a Wiccan ritual that's different for every person: knowing when the deity has arrived. If you truly desire the god or goddess to be present, you will usually sense a slight change in the energy of the circle after offering your invocation. Sometimes a candle burns a little brighter, or you feel a tingle in the back of your neck, or a sudden warm or cold breeze touches you.

If you feel the deity has *not* responded to your invocation, deliver it again, with greater feeling, perhaps embroidering it with further words of praise and longing. Repeat the deity's name, starting slowly and quietly and building in volume and intensity until you reach a peak, then allow a time of silence.

Then, if you still feel nothing, make a judgment call: Are you emotionally prepared to do spiritual work right now? Usually, when you sense no response, it is because your emotions are focused on something outside the circle. If you suspect this is the case, end the rite, go do something practical about whatever is bothering you and return when you are calmer.

If you do feel truly grounded and centered, continue with the ritual. You may find the deity is present, but is holding back to see what you're going to do.

In a meditation ritual, there is usually a time of silence, when you're not following a predetermined path. What happens during this time is unplanned and unpredictable. As with invocations, the experience will be different for every person. You might physically hear or see the deity, which can be disturbing if you're not expecting it. Less dramatically, your visualization may take on a life of its own, moving ahead with a story, like a waking dream. Try to remember what happens, but do not try to analyze or interpret while you are still within the meditation.

Occasionally you may find yourself in a visualization where you feel threatened or frightened. Deal with this the way you might deal with a nightmare: Take control of the situation, seeing yourself either overcoming whatever is disturbing or leaving the situation and going somewhere peaceful.

The Practical Side

Writing a ritual is like any other kind of writing: Five minutes of planning can save you hours. Before you plunge headlong into invocations and magical acts, answer these questions:

Who will be there? Perhaps this is for yourself alone, or for you and a partner. Perhaps it's for a group of Wiccan friends, or for members of a coven, or for a large festival.

If children will be present, you need to make sure the ritual is short enough for their attention spans, and includes appropriate ways for them to participate. If it's an open event and you don't know who will be there, play it safe by keeping the physical demands low. There is almost always someone with a bad knee or back, and there are few things more dampening to the spirit than to be forced to stand outside the circle while everyone else dances. If people with special talents, such as music or storytelling, will be present, think about whether those talents are appropriate for your ritual.

If more than one person will be taking part in the ritual, think about ways to split up the roles so that each interested person gets a chance to participate. It's better to include newcomers without singling them out. One way do to this is to have the whole group participate in some aspects of the ritual, such as chanting to raise energy or echoing the quarter calls.

Meditations are tricky, and should be led by the most experienced person, or perhaps the one with the most pleasant "ritual voice." If this is your first time leading a meditation for others, take it slow. I find it's usually necessary to allow one to three deep breaths between sentences, to let people get the idea. At some point in the meditation, the leader usually falls silent for a bit to allow the divine energy to communicate directly with the participants.

When will the ritual take place? This question has several aspects:

Time of day: Most rituals take place at night, but those honoring solar deities obviously should take place in sunlight. If you must do your personal rituals during the day (as I did when I worked the night shift), think about ways to introduce at least semi-darkness into your ritual space, either by going to a wooded place or by covering your windows.

If your ritual is to take place at or near a customary mealtime, you'll also need to make decisions about food. Many people prefer not to perform a ritual on a full stomach, since the lethargy associated with digestion can dampen a person's magical energy. Often, a group will hold a potluck supper after a ritual, to help everyone ground and to allow time to build social and community bonds among group members. This means deciding who will bring what, and perhaps planning some light pre-ritual snacks if the meal will be later than normal.

Day of the week: Some magical traditions give special significance to each day of the week. While there have been some imaginative attempts to translate this into a Celtic-oriented system, there is no evidence that the Celts used a seven-day calendar. So this comes down to practicality: If your rite is to take place on a weeknight, keep the event short enough so that participants can get home in time to get enough sleep for school or work the next day.

Significance of the date: If there is a special season or date associated with your chosen deity, you may want to consider this in planning your ritual. For instance, as discussed in the last chapter, the energy of Lugh is strongest in high summer, when his festival is held. This doesn't mean you shouldn't invoke Lugh in winter, but if you do so, you may find it valuable to add summer imagery to your invocations, meditations, and ritual decor.

Phase of the moon: While we don't know what religious signifi-
cance the Celts gave to the moon, many Wiccans associate various
energies with the phases of the moon, and you may want to con-
sider these when planning your timing:
First Quarter: beginnings, youth, love
Full Moon: growth, magic, fertility
Last Quarter: weeding, meditation, divination
Dark/New Moon: banishing, death, mourning

Where will you perform the ritual? In most cases, you need a
space where the participants can be assured of privacy and safety.

Outdoor rituals are wonderful, but need a little extra planning.
Besides ordinary physical precautions—warm clothing in winter,
bug repellent in summer—you need to make sure your site is legal
(many public parks are legally "closed" at sunset) and safely acces-
sible to all who are attending. Even experienced hikers can get lost
in the dark. When doing a ritual on public land, you may need to
modify your dress or equipment—for instance, substituting a wand
for an athame—so as not to break the law or appear threatening to
accidental passersby.

No matter what outdoor spot you're planning to use, visit it at
least once ahead of time, at the time of day when you'll be going
there for the ritual, and familiarize yourself with the route, the ordinary sights and sounds of the place, and any potential threats to
privacy and safety.

For personal or small group rituals, your home may be the best
place. Unless you live by yourself in an isolated place, you'll need to
consider how best to do your ritual without disturbing neighbors or
housemates. There is nothing wrong with speaking your invocations
in a whisper, or wearing scented oil instead of burning incense, if
these acts will help you to practice your religion while respecting
those among whom you dwell. Even if your neighbors are aware of
your faith and are understanding about it, be considerate of their
peace when deciding where to conduct your rituals.

For large rituals, or those that will be open to the public, you
may wish to consider renting space. This helps prevent some prob-

lems, because you don't run the risk of bringing unknown persons into your home. However, unless you can afford to absorb the charges yourself, you will have to charge admission to cover the rental costs, which may discourage some people from attending. You'll also need to be open with the owners of the space about your intentions. Many owners are reluctant to play host to anything Wiccan or Pagan. Good places to begin: Unitarian churches, New Age stores, campus Wiccan or Pagan organizations.

After you've found your space, make it temporarily yours—physically comfortable, suitable for your ritual purpose, and conducive to an atmosphere of worship and contemplation.

How will you achieve your ritual purpose? Rituals work best when it is clear what the purpose is and when the leaders have knowledge and understanding of the deities they're invoking. Participants should have the chance to add their own energy to the intent of the ritual, and to offer their own prayers or do their own magical work. The ritual should not keep people standing for hours, nor should it be so short that participants don't have time to enter a spiritual frame of mind.

It's a lot to manage, but it can be done. To do it, you'll need to refer once more to your research, and to the experiences you had while meditating.

Crafting the Ritual

Here's how we might create a ritual for Sulis, using the information gathered through our earlier research and meditation. Let's assume that we've chosen a time and place and invited some friends to take part.

To start, let's look at the invocation we used before. Does this still do an adequate job of describing Sulis and invoking her presence, taking into account the information we gathered during our meditations? We decide that it does, but that we need to add more information for the benefit of the other participants. While three verses seems like an appropriate number to offer in a Celtic rite, we add another that makes clear the reasons for the working:

Receive our worship
Bestow thy healing
Accept our gifts
Sulis!

We note that these four verses could be divided up among four participants if there are enough willing people available. We'll also ask all the participants to join in the calls of "Sulis!", as a way of pulling the group together toward the common goal of asking for the goddess's presence.

Next we look at the meditations we used to prepare ourselves. They're pretty long for a group, especially if there are going to be children present. By skipping the inner journey to and from the spring, we can shorten them significantly without losing a great deal of important information. We'll just have people visualize themselves already at the spring, and describe it in detail so that they can mentally place themselves there with us.

So far, so good. We've got the basics of a ritual in which we invoke Sulis and give participants an inner meditation experience of the ancient place where she was worshiped. Next we want to use the energy of the group to strengthen the connection to the goddess through a magical act, if possible an act consistent with what we know of Sulis' worship in ancient times.

Time to look at the history books again. What do we know people did to worship Sulis, and how can we echo those acts in modern times? Building stone sculptures or crafting lead curse tablets seems a little impractical. Offering coins to a spring seems like a more manageable act of worship.

If there's a hot spring in the vicinity, we could use that, or we might make do with a brook. But let's assume those aren't available. Instead, we decide to create a symbolic spring by borrowing a small tabletop fountain. We fill it with water, then add a little red and orange coloring to approximate the color of the spring water as it emerges from the earth. We place the fountain on our altar, with green plants beneath and beside it, and set it to bubble gently.

We'll also need to also assemble enough small coinage so that participants can each carry a coin into the ritual space, charging it with their own energy and intent, then drop it into the fountain with a prayer to the goddess at the end of the ritual. (We could ask each person to bring a coin, but even on this symbolic level I don't like to tell people they have to bring money for a ritual. I'd much rather gather up a bunch of pennies and give one to each participant as we're getting ready to begin.)

If each person goes up to the well, drops a coin in and offers up a prayer, that leaves a bit of a dull period for the rest of the participants. Perhaps there are musicians among those we've invited to attend. If they agree, we could ask them to choose a song suitable for this ritual, and to perform it at that point to help keep everyone focused.

We also decide on a chant and an accompanying movement for the raising of magical energy, which will harness the group's power to appeal to Sulis to grant our prayers. The movement I like to use is called "stirring the cauldron," and is popular at many public rites because, unlike dancing, it can be done by people who have difficulty walking or dancing. Participants join hands around the circle, then move each pair of hands in a (deosil) circular motion, as if stirring, moving more energetically as the power builds in the circle. We'll make sure we describe this action and show it to people before the ritual.

Finally, we compile a draft of the complete ritual, and make tentative assignments of parts.

Rite of Sulis

Preparation. On the altar are: a fountain surrounded by green plants, an incense burner, a large chalice of water, an athame, a wand, a platter with bread, and two candles. Each participant carries a coin.

Purification of Sacred Space with incense:

Let this place be cleansed of all that would cause harm or
fear! Let this be a place of purity, wisdom, and love!

Earth, Sea and Sky:
(touch staff to the floor three times)

Fruitful Land, to Thee we call to nourish and uphold us.
Blessed are we.

All: *Blessed are we.*
(with staff held upright, walk around the perimeter of circle)

Turbulent Sea, to Thee we call to surround and protect us.
Blessed are we.

All: *Blessed are we.*
(lift staff toward sky)

Radiant Sky, to Thee we call to guide and inspire us.
Blessed are we.

All: *Blessed are we.*

Calling of the Four Winds
(holding wand aloft at each direction)

Hear me, O Mighty One
Cool Wind of the East
Share with us your powers of inspiration
*   at this gateway between the worlds.*
Welcome, Wind of the East!

All: *Welcome, Wind of the East!*

Hear me, O Mighty One
Hot Wind of the South
Share with us your powers of action
*   at this gateway between the worlds.*
Welcome, Wind of the South!

All: *Welcome, Wind of the South!*

  Hear me, O Mighty One
  Misty Wind of the West
  Share with us your powers of love
   at this gateway between the worlds.
  Welcome, Wind of the West!

All: *Welcome, Wind of the West!*

  Hear me, O Mighty One
  Cold Wind of the North
  Share with us your powers of foundation
   at this gateway between the worlds.
  Welcome, Wind of the North!

All: *Welcome, Wind of the North!*

Invocation of Sulis:

  Warmth of the sun
  Mystery of the deep earth
  Power of the flowing water
  Sulis!

  Healing of ills
  Righting of wrongs
  Cleansing of impurity
  Sulis!

  Sight of the owl
  Hearing of the dolphin
  Speed of the snake
  Sulis!

  Accept our worship
  Bestow thy healing
  Accept our gifts
  Sulis!

Sulis, Giver of Healing, Righter of Wrongs! Of old thy sacred spring was a place of magic. Men and women of many nations came and prayed and sacrificed in thy name. Thy waters healed the sick and the grieving, consoled the angry and the fearful, and accepted the sacrifices of all.

Tonight we gather once more to praise thy name, to be healed and blessed, and to open our minds to thy wisdom. Sulis, we do call and invoke thee as ruler of the spring, to warm us with thy healing, and to teach us the wisdom that comes from the deepest heart of earth. Hail, Sulis!

All: *Hail, Sulis!*

Temple visualization:

Close your eyes and breathe deeply.

Imagine that you are in a place of shadows. You feel perfectly safe in this place.

Gradually the shadows clear, and you find that you are standing on a misty hillside. Ahead of you, to either side, you can see a great river, and around you are tree-filled swamps. You find that you are familiar with this place, and know that by walking straight ahead you will stay on dry ground.

Before you rises a low hill, and as you cross its gray-green summit you hear a bubbling flow of water. Following the sound, you find a rock from which hot water flows at a great pace, carving out a pool before flowing down to the river.

The cleft in the rock is colored a bright red-orange from the flow of hot water, and steam rises from the pool. This is the spring of Sulis.

Take a moment to concentrate on this magical place. When

*you are ready, we will proceed with the rite, but a part of
our minds will remain here, at the ancient sacred site.*

Raising energy ("stirring the cauldron"):

Sulis the healer, Sulis, renewer!

One of the ritual leaders approaches the altar and offers a coin. This
is the signal for the musicians to begin, and also lets others know
where to go and what to do. Each participant gets a chance to offer
a coin and prayer to Sulis, and to spend a brief moment in contemplation. When all are done, the musicians conclude their piece
and make their own offerings.

One of the ritual leaders takes up the chalice and dips her fingers
into it, then dabs water gently onto the hands, heart, and forehead
of the person to her left, saying:

May the waters of Sulis heal you and protect you.

Then the person who received this blessing takes the chalice and
turns to the left, and so on around the circle.

Closing meditation:

*Close your eyes once more and return to the pool of warm
water at the spring of Sulis. The hot air smells like fire and
like stone.*

*You may find that in your visualization, you have brought
something with you to offer to Sulis. Make this gift now, or
simply offer your thanks.*

*When you are ready, turn and walk back over the hill, away
from the river, past the tree-filled swamps. Soon you come to
the portal through which you entered this realm. Step
through it, and the doors close behind you. When you open
your eyes, you will fully return to this place and time.*

Farewell to Sulis:

> *O Ancient One, Sulis, Healer and Righter of Wrongs, know*
> *that we have gathered this night to honor thy name and*
> *praise thy powers. We thank you for these blessings, and for*
> *the healing and wisdom thou has granted us. Hail and*
> *farewell.*

All: *Hail and farewell.*

Dismissal of the Four Directions:

> *O Mighty Wind of the East (South, West, North)*
> *We thank thee for guarding this circle*
> *   and lending thy inspiration.*
> *Hail and farewell!*

All: *Hail and farewell!*

Land, Sea, and Sky (closing):
(touch staff to floor three times)

> *Fruitful Land, we thank thee for thy nourishment and*
> *upholding. Blessed are we.*

All: *Blessed are we.*
(with staff held upright, walk around the perimeter of circle widdershins)

> *Turbulent Sea, we thank thee for thy surrounding and*
> *protection. Blessed are we.*

All: *Blessed are we.*
(lift staff toward sky)

> *Radiant Sky, we thank thee for thy guidance and inspiration.*
> *Blessed are we.*

All: *Blessed are we.*

Final Notes

Ideally, the draft of a new ritual should be complete a couple of weeks before the event. This way, ritual leaders can devote time to preparing the space, preparing themselves, and memorizing their parts. While notes or scripts are common at Wiccan rituals, I find that as a participant, I am most effective at lending my energy when I know my role by heart—even when doing ritual by myself.

This planning process may seem over-elaborate for a solitary ritual. I follow it fairly closely for solo workings, because the experience is valuable when planning future rites involving the same deity. At the same time, a solitary practitioner can allow time during the ritual for the unexpected to happen. If you are seized by a spontaneous idea, a sudden desire to try something different, go ahead and put it into action!

In the rush of details accompanying a large group ritual—who's bringing what for potluck? where are the candles? who canceled at the last minute?—it is easy for the leaders to get distracted. When it's your turn to lead, be sure to set aside a little time alone to ground and center before the ritual begins. During the ritual, try to keep things flowing smoothly, but don't get upset if you or someone else makes a mistake. One of the gods' greatest gifts is a sense of humor!

After the ritual is over, remember to ground yourself thoroughly. Also, take the time to make some notes on what went well and what you might do differently next time.

FIVE

The Celtic
Creative
Tradition

It is one thing to read books—books like this one, and books of history and mythology—and begin to understand the Celtic peoples through the signs of their art and life. Far more personal and meaningful, however, is the work of bringing forth art and life of your own. If you never perform a ritual, you can still unleash your spirit through creating. In doing this you honor the many gods and goddesses whose attributes include craftsmanship, fertility, and skill.

The evidence left by Celtic artisans shows a rich and varied creativity, sophisticated in its simplicity. Their jewelry, metal decorations, shields, and helmets, often gathered in lavish burials, depict a common sinuous curve, a deliberate stylizing of human and animal features, and an appreciation for visual drama. The people who crafted these things are unknown, and little more is known about the elite few who owned them. Yet they have left a haunting glimpse of a world in which creativity was vital.

Creativity is vital to Wicca as well, for ours is a religion being constantly reinvented by the people who practice it. The experienced Wiccan needs no supplies to do an effective ritual, no One True Book on How to Worship, no authority figures prescribing the words and actions of our faith. The people who are doing the worshiping can craft all that they need by themselves. Indeed, the best rituals are often those that are created by a group of people to fill a need specific to them, with symbols each of them finds meaningful. As Wiccans have learned more about the modern origins of their religion, and the ways in which its founders adapted and combined material from the past, it has come to be said (in the words of journalist Margot Adler), "The real tradition of the Craft is creativity."

To develop this ability, and as a part of a balanced life, many Celtic Wiccans find one or more creative arts or crafts to pursue. Whether your creative path is a brand-new hobby or your life's work, it is a part of your spiritual development, and I urge you to make as much time as possible for the conscious practice of it. There is art in many things, and even mundane tasks can take on the glow of creativity if you can manage to look at them with a fresh eye and a conscious spirit. Simply put, creativity is that which engages your heart, opens your mind, and renews your spirit.

Is there something you do that you'd call creative? Do you do one thing just for the sake of creating, not to make money or make someone else happy? Do you feel relaxed after working in your garden, or sewing curtains? Do you feel a warm sense of accomplishment when you put your whole mind and heart into teaching a child or building a fence? These feelings can help point the way toward your creative outlet.

Creativity has value beyond its spiritual significance, and brings its own joys. Art, music, dance, crafts, and many other activities can encourage relaxation and renewal, allowing us to stretch our minds and hearts, to learn and grow more skilled at our own pace, and to bring fresh energy back to the rest of our lives. For a Celtic Wiccan the artistic impulse is specifically understood to be a gift of the gods, and its expression a spiritual act.

For some, creativity is a way of life in itself—one not without sacrifices, surely, but a vital and often-envied path. Others manage to find and take joy in creatively approaching everything from household tasks to computer-engineering jobs.

Several years ago, I took up a musical instrument for the wrong reason (to please someone else) and ended up gaining far more than I expected from the experience. I have been lucky enough to find a like-minded group of people, who play together with a specific goal of having fun. We learn new pieces and techniques, extending our skills and rising to the challenge of public performances—but the fun is the important part. I know I'm not the only one who's shown up at rehearsal saying, "I need this today!"

As part of your exploration of Celtic spirituality, I encourage you to consciously incorporate more creativity into your life. If you don't currently have a creative pursuit, begin to think about something you'd like to do, make, sing, or learn. Perhaps it's time to rediscover something you learned in childhood, or manifest an idea that won't leave the back of your head. Listen to suggestions from the people around you, but make sure the creative path you choose is truly yours.

If you're starting something new, it's important to remember that the process is more meaningful than the product. So don't get upset with yourself or give up when you can't do great work right away. The effort of practicing, of working at a skill until you learn it, is essential to the personal growth that comes with creativity. Find joy in it and keep doing it, adding to your knowledge and reimagining your work each time. As time passes, you'll notice your skills improving of their own accord.

If you already have a creative outlet, think about whether there is something new you want to try. There's something useful and humbling about being a beginner, and a wonderful feeling of accomplishment when you realize you've left that beginner stage behind! Or perhaps there's some way in which you can push yourself further within your creative field—a bigger project, a bolder performance, a new way of looking at things. Stretch yourself, and enjoy the feeling.

Try this: Go through an entire day approaching each event with the intent of creating beauty and doing your work with skill and attention to detail. You may find that singing makes the housework go more quickly, that alertness and ability make you safer behind the wheel, that you can do your job or your schoolwork at a higher and more conscious level, or use creative thinking to understand a child's misbehavior.

It takes energy to sustain this, doesn't it? Yet it's a useful exercise, and worth repeating from time to time.

The Celtic Visual Style

Because the objects that survive are almost all of metal and stone, we have lost a great deal of information about how the Celts worked in wood, cloth, and bone. Because they transmitted information about their arts through word of mouth rather than written language, we have lost a great deal of information about the stories, poems, songs, dances, and crafts that were important to them. Yet their surviving artifacts give us clues to the things they thought beautiful and meaningful.

Ancient descriptions of the Celts emphasize their love of color and display. No tasteful understatement for them! Whenever possible, the Celtic artisan preferred not to make an item plain if it could be decorated. This artistic and personal style was not a mere show of wealth, but a conscious symbolic language that we are at a loss to fully understand. Celtic artisans followed a recognizable form in which lines curve and flow, animals leap and people and gods stare right back at their viewers. They also held themselves to strict standards of craftsmanship, decorating even the undersides of clothing pins and the bottoms of statues—places not meant to be displayed.

One of the chief vehicles for this bold style was the Celts themselves. Even very early in the Celtic period, weavers were creating garments with striped and checked patterns and bright colors. Scientists have studied a few Celtic cloth scraps that show such decorations as geometric patterns, beading, embroidery, and even a "cloth of gold" effect with thin strips of gold wound around thread. Later

Irish tales describe the figures of mythology as people who took care of their appearance, bathing every day and anointing themselves with scented oils. Celtic women put crimson dye on their nails and wore vegetable colorings as makeup. Both sexes wore their hair long and in braids, decorated with headbands or beads. Warriors decorated their bodies for battle with "woad," a vegetable dye that makes blue markings similar to tattoos (except the woad wears off in a few weeks). Cloaks were fastened with bronze, iron, or gold pins, often large and elaborate.

Furniture, clothing, and horse trappings all bore decorations if the owner could afford them. From Celtic cultures we even have a few spectacular hoards of silver and gold plates and cups, elaborately embellished with scenes of gods and the hunt.

The Celts' style was intensely a part of their identity. When Celtic tribes were exposed to other cultures' art through trade, they adapted themes and patterns from the new influences, but seldom copied them directly.

For all their love of putting on a good show, the Celts rarely depicted themselves in their art, perhaps because of a religious taboo. A few statues and masks indicate real people or gods, but animals, plants, and abstract themes were far more common. Masks of human faces do appear on ceramics and metalwork, reflecting the power accorded to the head in Celtic belief, but the heads themselves are usually drawn in simplistic style, with little attempt to portray a real person. Sometimes heads and faces are hidden within other designs as a sort of visual pun; other times they are drawn with such exaggerated lines as to appear cartoonish (scholars group these items under a style they call "Disney"). Celtic depictions of animals were usually stylized, the animal's form molded to the curving lines of the artist's design. As Roman art forms, which emphasized realistic portrayal of people and gods, became more prevalent, a few pieces show distinct signs of combining the two styles.

The "knotwork" style so often associated with Ireland didn't fully develop until well into the Christian period. While some Celtic patterns flowed and twisted around themselves, the lines tended to be more curved than bent. The curving Celtic style lent itself to spirals and *triskeles* (triple spirals), along with serpentine and leaf-based patterns, often tripled in some way.

Music

We know some of the arts that were important in Celtic cultures—metalworking, weaving, jewelry making, and stone carving, to name a few. Others, such as music, we must guess at from the stories told by later cultures, and from our knowledge of similar groups of people.

The evidence we do have strongly suggests a society where music was respected and loved. Several pottery and metal objects depict trumpet-players. One altar dedicated to the "young god" Maponus equates him with Apollo Cithareodos, the Greek patron of harpers. One of the Roman historians, Diodorus Siculus, writing in about 21 B.C.E., describes the "composers of verses . . . singing to instruments comparable to a lyre, applaud some, while they vituperate others." This is an early indication of the role of the bards, whose satires were feared and whose praises were courted by the powerful. The Celts may have recognized music and poetry as having spiritual powers of their own, powers many modern musicians recognize in one way or another.

Music played another role as well, that of the trumpet sounding the call to battle. A Roman historian writes of the dreadful noise the Celts' trumpeters made, and four bronze horns—ceremonial or military, we shall never know which—were discovered near an Irish lake. Only one of them is on display, and it still can be played! The sound is low and not very melodic, but certainly enough to communicate signals or salute the gods.

Extending Your Creative Spirit

You can, and should, enjoy the benefits of creativity in whatever way best expresses your own ideas. By all means listen to others' suggestions, but give yourself the freedom to say "no" to ideas that aren't right for you. Having said that, I'm going to offer some ideas for experimenting with the Celtic artistic spirit in your own creative work.

It is never too late to work on the fundamentals. Professional musicians play scales every day. Your most successful flights of creativity will come from a thorough understanding of your craft, of how to perform its most basic tasks. Only when you have mastered the rules can you confidently break them. Whatever you're doing—no matter how pedestrian or familiar—is worth doing at the highest level of quality you can muster, with the full energy of your mind and heart.

Doing something creative is better than doing nothing. So your band doesn't have any gigs this month? Play at a school for free, just to keep in practice. Still trying to come up with an idea for a novel? Write something, anything. A really good letter to the bank, or a poem for your five-year-old niece, might turn out to be just the jump-start you needed. Or, if the well of inspiration in one field seems to have run dry, it might be time to experiment with a new one. Consider especially the arts of the Celts—metalworking, sculpture, weaving, poetry.

Seek out teachers and listen to them. They may not be the ones who win big prizes or get written up in national magazines. The mentors you need are the ones who consistently create beautiful, interesting, meaningful work, whose ultimate pride and pleasure is in the craft itself and not in the opinions of others. Find them by asking others, by looking for work that moves and awakens you, by reading books and magazines and Web sites, by learning everything you can about your creative field. When you have found these people, treat them with respect, ask them intelligent questions, and really listen to the answers. Later, when it's your turn to teach, do so with kindness and patience.

Work with other creative people. A team—whether it be a temporary group set up to pull off one project, or an ongoing partnership in creativity—can offer the opportunity for members to feed off one another's ideas, with a result that can be more than the sum of its parts. Working on an equal basis with others brings you face to face with your own values and goals, and provides important lessons in respect and in getting out of your own way.

If you don't know other creative people, consider starting a group—a weekly writing critique, a dance cooperative, a drum circle. Instead of just letting egos bump up against one another, settle on a common goal and work toward it together, agreeing that all your expressions are worthy of respect. If one group doesn't work out, try another. Years later, you may not remember how many paintings you made or poems you wrote. But you'll remember the moments when you learned something new, or gave something of value to another.

Find a role model. Make a point of exposing yourself to the work of the people you consider the best in your field, even those whose approaches differ from yours. A role model is different from a teacher, and can even be someone who is dead. Experiencing such people's work may make you jealous, but please don't let it stop you from doing what you do. Enjoy the beauty and craftsmanship of the experts for its own sake. Then use the experience to motivate you toward better and more meaningful work of your own.

Be a role model. Let the people around you know that you do something creative. Many people, especially young people, need to know that this is part of a balanced life, and one of the best ways to learn this is by seeing it happen in the life of someone you respect. Let the people of your family and community see you struggle to improve your skills. Let them see you finding joy and fresh energy in the creative work you do. Answer their questions and encourage them to find their own creative paths.

Stay positive. Remember that you are doing this for fun, even if it's also your work. Some days it may be an effort to find the pleasure in your creativity, but it is an effort worth making. When you find yourself becoming stressed or anxious about this part of your life, be ruthless as you make the necessary changes to put your craft in a better mental and emotional place. Remember to stop and congratulate yourself on each small piece you accomplish, and give yourself serious time to bask in the pleasure of completing a big project. If you're working with others, encourage them by focusing on the things they do right.

Creativity in Spiritual Life

Your spiritual life is also an excellent outlet for creativity, for the gods of the Celts are particularly receptive to gifts of poetry, music, art, and other creative works. There are many Wiccan rituals out there, but only you can craft the ones that express your own spiritual relationships.

Your journeys into Celtic history and Wiccan religion will also provide a wealth of material, from the stories of Irish and Welsh myth to the historical artifacts, with their mysteries and their unique style. When you find yourself getting creatively "stuck," try incorporating a theme or idea from the ancients—make a line into a curve, find a theme that lends itself to heads and faces, strike a bolder note.

When life gets busy and hectic, when a crisis is erupting around you, it may seem easy to move your creativity to one side, to say, "I don't have time for this now." Push yourself to make the time, for this may be the time when you need your creative side the most. Art is a time-honored way of expressing feelings and working through difficulties. It is also a way of connecting with the side of you that is most open to the gods, and you may find them speaking through your creative work, or you may find yourself gaining sudden insights while in the meditative state that such work can induce.

Through creativity we can receive inspiration from the gods, and offer them our gifts in return. Creativity is also a way of building community with others who share your beliefs. If you are not now active in your local Pagan community, consider making a small contribution of creative work—a poem for the local Pagan or New Age newsletter, a song for the "bardic circle" at a festival. As you grow in expertise and confidence, consider offering your gifts in the form of workshops or starting a group to teach others your art. Finally, at the ceremonies and seasons when gift-giving is customary, Pagans and Wiccans often exchange gifts from their own hands.

At this point many people will hold back from offering their work to the world, or even from creating at all. "I'm not good enough" is a persistent feeling, difficult to dislodge. It's easy to stifle your best work for fear of others' opinions. Sometimes other people *will* dislike your work, or even belittle it. What they cannot do is touch the spirit that went into creating your work, the spirit that is yours alone. If they don't understand it, perhaps it's because they have limitations of their own, or because their insecurities lead them to believe they must belittle others. If your work is real and true, keep your head held high. Just by doing your creative work, you are doing more than many people ever manage.

Rítual: The Forge

To infuse your creative work with spiritual meaning, one effective technique is to create sacred space and perform your work within it. In this ritual, the artist calls upon the Celtic smith-god, who presides over the mystical process of transforming raw metal into something useful, powerful, beautiful, or perhaps all three. Those who have tried metalsmithing will tell you it is as much an art as a science, a demanding craft that carries its own dangers and encourages in its practitioners a careful and thoughtful outlook.

We do not know what the ancient Celts called this god. We know he was worshiped widely, for we have bronze figures and pottery shards that show a god attired in a cap and belted tunic, with one shoulder bare, surrounded by tools such as anvils and tongs. He's clearly a different being from the hammer-god, Sucellos, shown with tools of farming and winemaking. For the purpose of this ritual, we shall call the smith-god Gofannon (pronounced "go-VAN-un"), a name associated with the divine smith in later Welsh mythology.

For this ritual, your worship and workshop spaces need to be the same. If your artwork can be moved into your regular sacred space, do so; otherwise, you'll need to find some way to make your art space (garden, dance floor, music studio) connected somehow to your spiritual path. Arrange to be alone or with others who will participate in the ritual and use it for their own creative work. Set aside one part of your space—a windowsill, or even just a bit of the ground—as an altar, and mark it in some way. Choose a stone— any small stone from outdoors will do, though a smooth one is better—and place it on your altar.

Assemble in this place the tools and raw materials for what you plan to create—beads, oils, dance shoes, musical instruments, seeds, paints, herbs, wood, whatever. Go over the process of creation in your head and make sure you have everything you'll need to at least get started. If your ritual garb is suitable for your art, wear it; otherwise, wear whatever you would normally wear for your creative pursuit.

When you are ready to begin, ground and center yourself thoroughly. If your art is a physically demanding one, take a few moments to stretch the muscles you will use.

Cast a circle thus:

(touching the ground)

> *Fruitful Land, source of all that is, your creative force awes and inspires us. I honor you and ask your aid.*

(inscribing the circle deosil with your footsteps or outstretched hands)

> *Powerful Sea, ever flowing and ebbing, your endurance turns hard edges to smooth curves and fosters teeming life. I honor you and ask your aid.*

(reaching upward)

> *Radiant Sky, source of warmth and water, your light illuminates beauty and truth. I honor you and ask your aid.*

Call the quarters thus:

> *Spear of the East, fill this circle with knowledge,*
> *that I may practice my craft with skill and honor.*
> *Sword of the South, fill this circle with passion,*

that I may put my whole heart into that which I create.
*   Cauldron of the West, fill this circle with love,*
that my work may wash me clean of fear and unhappiness
*   Stone of the North, fill this circle with strength,*
that I may challenge myself to greater things.

Go to your altar and hold your stone in both hands as you invoke the god. Visualize him before you: a strong and quiet man, not too young, wearing a beard and a thick belted tunic, trousers, cap, and boots. As he looks directly at you, he seems to challenge you. He may hold a pair of tongs in his hand, and wear an iron *torc* around his neck.

Gofannon, keeper of the sacred forge,
Whose weapons strike true,
Whose hands create beauty,
Whose fire brings forth strength,
Whose art turns stone of the earth,
*   into graceful iron and shining steel,*
I call and beseech you, Gofannon,
Lend your strength to my hand,
Your sight to my eye,
Your art to all that is within me.
Hail, Gofannon!

Holding the stone, summon up all the thoughts and criticisms that might come your way and keep you from putting your full creative spirit into your work. Thoughts like "This isn't good enough," "My teacher won't like it," "Nobody really looks at this stuff," "My friends will think I'm weird." Focus for a few moments until your mind is filled with these thoughts. Then gather them up and mentally squeeze them into the stone. Hold the stone tightly, feeling all your fear, all your self-doubts flow into the stone. Place the stone on the altar.

Stone of Gofannon, I charge you to absorb all
negative thoughts and criticisms of this my work. If

others' words reject me, they will not stop my hand.
If my own doubts rise up to defeat me, they will not
stop my imagining. If I find my work is lacking, I
will study and learn from it, and try again.

Remain in meditation for a few moments, then, keeping your mind open to ideas and inspirations, begin your work. It may feel difficult to do your artwork after such a buildup. Try not to place expectations on yourself. You are not here to do your best work, but to explore and experiment. With Gofannon's help you are free to transform the raw materials before you, materials that include your own ideas and skills. And if all that happens is a chance to learn what *doesn't* work, that in itself is valuable.

Start with something small, perhaps something you already know how to do. When it is done, take note of your own accomplishment, for your own praise will help spur you onward. Don't think too much about what you're doing. It may even help to imagine yourself as a channel for ideas and inspirations from the inner world. Take note of your own emotions as you work, and consciously give yourself messages of confidence and openness to new ideas. If you are crafting something tangible, do not destroy your mistakes until after the ritual is over.

Stay here as long as you can. Take breaks in between projects or pieces of a project, and try meditating with deep breaths, making your mind as blank as possible.

When you feel it is time to depart, return to the altar. Go over your creative session in your mind, and take special note of the things you learned or accomplished. In your own words, describe what you did, and offer Gofannon your thanks for the ideas and experiments you have made during this time.

Keeper of the Forge,
You have been by me in my hour of inspiration
You have instilled me with your creative fire
And though I still have much to learn
I will keep your magic by me.

I thank you and honor you.
Hail and farewell.

Bid farewell to the directions thus:

Stone of the North, I thank you, for that which I have done and that which I have learned. Hail and farewell.

Cauldron of the West, I thank you for that which I have done and that which I have learned. Hail and farewell.

Sword of the South, I thank you for that which I have done and that which I have learned. Hail and farewell.

Spear of the East, I thank you for that which I have done and that which I have learned. Hail and farewell.

And finally, take up the circle:

(reaching upward)

Radiant Sky, I thank you for your illumination. Hail and farewell.

("erasing" the energy of the circle with your feet or hands as you move widdershins around it)

Powerful Sea, I thank you for your protection. Hail and farewell.

(touching the earth)

Fruitful Land, I thank you for your growth. Hail and farewell.

You may choose to keep the stone in your creative space, or symbolically rid yourself of self-defeating thoughts by casting it into a forest or body of water.

Ritual: The Sacrifice of Art

In Celtic religion, as in many ancient religions, much meaning was attached to sacrifice. We have abundant evidence of animal sacrifices among the Celts, and some of human sacrifices. In modern Wicca, the sacrifice of a living animal is of course considered repugnant, and some people even object to cutting a branch off a living tree to make a wand. Yet there is one form of Celtic votive offering that is entirely suited for modern worship: the sacrifice of art.

Throughout the Celtic world, scholars have remarked on the apparently widespread practice of offering handcrafted objects, often of highest quality and craftsmanship, into rivers, lakes, ponds, and marshes, or burying them in the earth. We cannot know for sure what this act signified to the people who performed it, but the evidence seems to support the idea that these offerings were sacrifices to the gods and goddesses of their worship. Some of the items were never used before being cast into the water.

While most of the objects excavated from such burials are weapons, Celtic worshipers also offered the products of more down-to-earth emblems of prosperity—grain, for example, and animals grown for food. In some bogs in Scotland and Ireland, archaeologists have even found offerings of butter! No doubt many other offerings, made from organic substances like wood or cloth, have been lost to time.

Historian and archaeologist Barry Cunliffe describes a Celtic world where tribes came together to make the great offerings of weapons and gold, but where individuals and small communities carried out offerings on a regular basis on their own. In times of difficulty—war, bad harvests, disease—the tribes might have felt a need to better cement their relationships with the gods and goddesses, and increased their offerings accordingly.

The following is an imaginative adaptation in Wiccan terms of the act of sacrificing an object of craftsmanship and value. It should not in any way be taken as a reflection of the attitudes or rituals the ancient Celts might have brought to such an act, for those are unknown to us.

This ritual takes considerable time and energy to arrange, and might be best performed on an annual basis. It is also suited for major events and times of great need—a personal or community crisis, perhaps, or the commemoration of a death or other rite of passage. The occasion will also help determine whether you perform this rite alone or in a group.

Let us say that you are performing this ritual alone, to ask the gods for help in dealing with a personal transition. Perhaps, by choice or circumstance, you are going to move to an unfamiliar place. Though it may be for the best, such a situation is often fraught with fear and uncertainty, and you seek divine help in smoothing the way for you to settle happily in the new place.

Following the ritual-construction system outlined in the last chapter, it is important to do everything necessary in your daily life to deal with the issue. In this case, sorting through your belongings, researching the new area, and making plans for a return trip to your old home might be reasonable steps.

Second, choose a goddess or god whom you will honor with your offering. Doing some research into Celtic deities, you find Nehalennia, a goddess who governed sea journeys and protected mariners, merchants, and travelers.

Prepare as you would for any major ritual. Study the art and associations of the chosen goddess, and look for ways to bring yourself closer to her through your senses. You might notice, for example, that Nehalennia was always pictured with a dog, probably as a protective emblem. This might lead you to spend time with dogs in the days leading up to the ritual. Give yourself time for grounding and meditation, and prepare yourself by invoking the goddess in a meditation ritual, so that you are connected with her energy and can seek her guidance on how best to worship her.

At the same time, though, begin constructing your offering of art. This should be the finest and best that you can create. This should not be something purchased, but something into which you have put your own energy and creativity. In some cases the best solution is to buy or find a plain object that you will then decorate. Consider also the fact that you will be offering this in a place of nature, and use organic materials in preference to pollutants such as plastics.

Some ideas for offerings: a loaf of bread, a song, a decorated piece of pottery, a handcrafted knife, an item of handmade clothing, a poem, a story, a piece of jewelry, home-grown flowers or fruit, a painting, a clay sculpture, a hand-tooled leather belt, a set of handmade candles.

Whatever you choose, let it be something that you will enjoy creating, so that you feel motivated to add more energy to it. Give to this object the best of your imagination, planning, design, and skill. Your goddess and your goal deserve no less! If you find yourself searching for themes or ideas, consider incorporating symbols of the goddess, of dogs, of journeys. Reflect on the Celtic visual style, and give your work something of that curve and splendor. Do not rush your work, but do not hold onto it too long, either, obsessing over the piece when it is finished.

If you are offering something you have written, make a single good copy. Destroy any computer files, rough drafts, or practice drawings you made, so that your final work is the only version in existence. You can go back and redo the same project later, but this one work will be offered as a true sacrifice, a gift to the goddess that is all the more meaningful because you will give your finest work, knowing you will not see it again.

Next you need to locate a physical setting for your votive offering, for this is one form of ritual which must be done outdoors. If there is an ocean or body of water near where you live, identify a secluded spot along it, one to which you have easy and legal access, and in which there is a sufficient depth of water to swallow up your offering. If you can do so safely, consider making your offering from a boat or bridge, since both are associated with ancient water-offerings. Find a time when you are unlikely to be disturbed in your chosen spot. If you do not live near water, dig an offering-pit in a secluded spot, and scatter water over it as part of your ritual.

Before you do your ritual, you will need to write your own invocation to Nehalennia. You may prefer to memorize invocations and other ritual parts, but leave yourself open to the possibility that you will be inspired with new words in the moment.

Choose a time for your ritual based on your schedule and the times you can be alone in your chosen location. Dress sensibly for the weather and location, but if possible wear at least one piece of meaningful clothing or jewelry (perhaps a pendant shaped like Nehalennia's sacred dog?) to mark the occasion as special. Bring minimal ritual equipment. A wand and some wine or juice would be reasonable, along with your offering. Candles are nice, but in a windy location a lantern or flashlight may be a more practical source of whatever light you need.

Ground and center before you depart for your rite, and proceed slowly and deliberately on your route, for this is a sacred procession, even if you're the only one who knows it. Take time to carefully survey your ritual spot, noting your level of privacy and doing whatever you need to feel safe here, so that you may focus on the intention of your ritual.

Salute the land, sea, and sky, and acknowledge the four directions. Then offer your invocation to Nehalennia, praising the goddess and asking that she accept your offering.

Hold your offering in your hands. If it is a poem or story, put your heart into the reading of it, slowly and with all the skill you can manage. If your offering is a song or sonata or dance, perform it with passion. It may seem a little silly at first to be delivering this impassioned performance outside by yourself. Yet you're not by yourself. The goddess is here to receive your offering, and it is therefore important to strive for the highest standards of your art.

Take time to admire the craftsmanship of your work, noticing not the mistakes but the best qualities. Then, when you are ready, deliver a prayer in your own words, asking Nehalennia to accept your gift, to protect you on your passage to a new life, and to grant you good fortune once you get there.

Then place your offering in the water. Wade out if you need to, to make sure it won't come floating back to shore. Offer some final words, perhaps along these lines:

> This I offer to you, Nehalennia,
> Freely and willingly
> With praise for your beauty and grace,

Your strength and protection.
Let your hound walk by me
As I make my journey,
Let the storms abate,
Let me reach my goal,
This I pray, O Nehalennia.

Bid the goddess farewell, and end the ritual in an orderly fashion. Return to your ordinary life, knowing that you have made a great sacrifice to obtain the favor of the goddess.

This ritual is easily adapted for a family, or for a different circumstance such as a passage into or out of marriage, the birth of a baby, the founding of a business or coven, or even the beginning of a major creative project.

Get Creative!

The process of creating, learning, and growth is a reflection of the cycle of fertility. Many ancient customs are concerned with making land, livestock, and people more fertile, for such fruitfulness meant the difference between mere survival and prosperity. Even today, many Wiccan rites have fertility aspects to them, as you'll see in the chapter on the Wheel of the Year.

You may not be concerned with childbirth or agriculture at this point in your life, but you can still find meaning in fertility rites by applying their energy to your creative spirit. This force is a powerful source of personal renewal, allowing you to bring fresh perspective to everyday life.

In this chapter, I have given only the barest outline of the fascinating history of Celtic art. I encourage you to explore this further, for their art is one of the few ways the Celts communicated directly with us about the symbols and sacred figures important to their worship. Besides informing your understanding of the Celts, the study of their art is fulfilling simply because it brings you face-to-face with beauty, mystery, and skill.

SIX

Celtic Wicca
in Daily Life

Having chosen a Celtic Wiccan path, it would be pleasant to live all day in service to the gods and goddesses, able to spend each waking moment on creative and soul-renewing acts. Alas, most of us find our energy taken up by the work of sustaining ourselves and our families.

So how to keep your faith alive while restarting the computer, worrying about the brake fluid, and juggling the kids' schedules? Fortunately for us, Celtic Wicca is a vital and creative religion. Our gods and goddesses can be found even in fluorescent-lit offices and concrete buildings. Our values can and should be expressed in every part of our lives.

As you learn more about Celtic Wicca, you may begin to see its values seep into your day-to-day interactions. Casual friends may notice little change, but you'll know that this wisdom is helping to motivate you. Don't consider my ideas the last word. In the end, like your art and your rituals, the expression of spiritual virtues in your life must be truly your own creation.

At Work

If you work outside the home, chances are your employer will not appreciate blatant declarations of Wiccan faith. While religious discrimination is illegal in the United States, many Wiccans have found that employers who disapprove of their faith can easily come up with grounds for dismissal or make their work lives miserable. Even owning your own business requires discretion, because you're usually not in a position to risk offending any potential customer.

Yet work is where we spend many of our waking hours, forming social networks and sustaining our physical lives. It would be foolish to pretend you can switch off your spirit at the factory gate or in the mall parking lot. How then can you manifest the Celtic virtue of truth, while maintaining a productive and stable work situation?

First, you need not hide all symbols of your faith. While pentagrams are likely to draw the wrong sort of attention, Celtic symbols are quite common, yet have meanings that go far beyond their beauty. The *triskele* (triple spiral), for example, can be found carved on the walls of the ancient stone tomb at Newgrange, Ireland, and symbolizes the power of the number three in ancient Celtic religion. I wear this symbol frequently on jewelry as an acknowledgment of the three realms (land, sea, and sky) and their related qualities (nurturance, protection, and inspiration).

If you study Celtic poetry or art, you'll notice that the Celts delighted in obscuring the truth to all but the select few who know the secret. Swirling spirals may resolve themselves into birds or trees if you look long enough; in the later writings, a long, complex poem may be clearly symbolic of grand concepts, yet remain a mystery to modern scholars. To another Celtic Wiccan, my *triskele* earrings might be the cue for a quiet conversation; to everyone else, they're just jewelry.

Of course, you needn't wear any symbol of your religion, and in some jobs such items are unsafe or prohibited. If you have any personal space at all in your work environment, make it a place of renewal, a spiritual "home." If you have a desk of your own, or an office, use the opportunity to discreetly acknowledge your faith and sustain your spirit. Caring for a plant can help remind you of the relationship between Wiccans and nature. A special stone, chosen in a place of nature, can help ground you in a workplace full of stress. If all the space you have to yourself is a locker or file drawer, decorate the inside with a picture of a meaningful landscape. Whenever you see the picture, take just a second to intentionally gaze at it, to remind you of your true self as you go through each workday.

Such workplace reminders help keep us grounded. They tell us that the gods and goddesses, and the powers of nature, will be here long after this crunch is over, this crisis resolved. Those powers are available to us even in an inhospitable workaday world. If you or your office has need of a particular virtue—creativity, let us say, or honor— you can magically charge your workplace objects before bringing them in, asking that they lend that virtue to their environment.

Objects of power needn't even be visible to others. I find that mentally surrounding myself with the powers of land, sea, and sky before a tense discussion helps me to act more effectively. When arguing before an executive who often viewed my ideas negatively, I envisioned a warrior's shield protecting my upper body, and found myself better able to respond when challenged.

This workplace ritual is an adaptation of a common Wiccan rite, in which you charge a "house stone" to absorb negative energies in your home. The "work stone" will perform the same function in your place of work.

Quick Work-Stone Rite

Find a black or dark stone, of whatever size will suit your work space. Buy the stone if need be, but you may prefer to find it outside, shaped and cleansed by the powers of nature.

At your home altar or sacred place, ground and center yourself as you prepare for your ritual. (If you are particularly angry about events in your workplace, take extra time to let the earth absorb that energy, which otherwise will deflect the purpose of this rite.) Call on a god or goddess whom you associate with your work. In this example, I'll invoke Sucellos. As a god of agricultural productivity, his influence may easily be extended to govern the work that gives us our means of survival.

Still holding the stone, offer it up to Sucellos:

> Sucellos, Hammer-God
> You who protect the fields and vines
> Fill this stone with thy protection
> That it may absorb
> All energy that would harm me.

If you have specific requests, such as keeping competitors from harming your business, keeping distractions from sapping your energy, or protecting your job from downsizing, speak them aloud. End with:

> Let this be done
> With harm to none.

Hold the stone in your receptive hand (left if you're right-handed), and stroke it with your other hand as you chant:

> Stone of midnight, magic spell
> All that would do harm, dispel
> That I my work may do full well.

Repeat the chant for several minutes, turning the stone over so that you thoroughly imbue it with your own energy and the blessings of Sucellos. When you are done, thank the god and end your rite. At your workplace, install the stone in an inconspicuous location; as you set it down, ask it to absorb the negative energies of that space. In six months to a year, you may sense that the stone is "full"; simply return it to the place where you found it and perform the rite again with another one.

At School

If you're in school, it may not feel like an enviable life to you right now, but it is. The chief object of your life is gaining knowledge, a goal dear to the hearts of ancient Celts. Roman historians reported that Druids of the first century studied for twenty years before taking up their priesthoods, memorizing everything rather than writing it down. (And you think *you've* got a workload!)

Those Druids and bards studied many of the same things people study today—language, poetry, history, music, art, and healing. Centuries before them, Neolithic tribes showed an impressive knowledge of astronomy and mathematics in the stone observatories they left behind. Celtic warriors, of course, studied the arts of war. (And not just the men, either. In many later stories, there's a running theme of male heroes who get their training from women.)

If you're studying history or art or Gaelic language, it's pretty easy to see how your schoolwork and your religion help each other. But what if you're studying computer programming, auto repair, or radiology? Remember that the ancient Celts valued technology highly. Long before they came in contact with the Romans, Celtic peoples developed complex metalworking techniques. Smiths, the most technical workers of their era, were valued members of society whose work had mystical significance.

In learning the highest technologies available to modern culture, you are fulfilling a truly Celtic impulse. It's also a common impulse among modern Wiccans. There's no accurate census of Wiccans, who are too independent-minded to have one central organization. However, many surveys and observers have noted a high percentage of technical workers. (Including me: I make my living producing Web sites.) Anthropologist Tanya Luhrmann noted this tendency in her book *Persuasions of the Witch's Craft*, a study of modern Wiccans and ceremonial magicians. Her explanation strikes me as having the ring of truth.

Many magicians become computer programmers because they need a job. They are often people who are not driven by a career

choice; they are often bright. The natural arena to which such a
person might turn for a well-paid job . . . is the computer industry.

No matter what your field of study, Celtic honor demands that you learn it well so that you may practice it wisely for the good of others. Honor also requires giving true service to yourself as well as others. That means learning enough to be a true practitioner of your craft or disseminator of wisdom—not just memorizing enough to get through the test.

It is through being tested that we find our true strengths. Those who wished to join the Fianna, the Irish warrior bands, had to pass a rigorous set of physical tests. Those who wished to call themselves bards had to recite long stretches of history-poetry from memory. Your tests may be different from theirs, but their feelings were probably very similar to yours.

Spell for Test-Takers

First, my not-so-mystical secret: By all means study, but also get eight hours' sleep the night before the test. Cramming all night may get the information into your head, but it won't help you present it coherently or solve problems well. Without a written tradition, the Celts valued memory highly; yours will function best, pulling out half-remembered facts and obscure connections, when you are rested.

Sleep not only restores the body and mind, but also the spirit. Many cultures regard sleep as a halfway point between life and death. Irish texts from the early Christian period refer to a ritual called *imbas forosnai*, in which the practitioner makes a sacrifice of meat and prays to the gods until going to sleep.

The evening before a test, try this very brief spell: Hold an apple in your dominant hand as you invoke a god or goddess particularly associated with your field of study. In this example, I'll call on Brigid, whose triple patronage (smithcraft, healing, and poetry) brings many students under her influence. Ground and center, then offer this invocation with as much sincere feeling as you can.

Brigid, Goddess of the Flame
Goddess of Inspiration, Goddess of Craft
Fill my hands with skill
My mind with clarity
And my heart with courage.
Restore and renew me tonight,
And be with me tomorrow.
Accept this offering
As a token of my thanks.

Take one bite of the apple, then set it down and close your eyes. Meditate on the goddess's blessings, feeling them flowing into you for as long as you can taste the apple. Thank the goddess as you open your eyes. Leave the apple outside, preferably near a tree, and go to bed.

Raising Children

I'm not a parent, so it would be highly presumptuous of me to tell you how to raise your kids. A growing number of Wiccan and Pagan parents have shared their experience and wisdom for the benefit of other parents, and I'll list some of their books at the end of this one. Still, I can point to some ways in which Celtic Wicca may help build a stronger, more enjoyable family life.

First, however, you need to make an important decision: Do you want to raise your child as a Wiccan? If you're sincere in your faith, your first answer might be "Of course!" Yet there are good reasons to think twice. The decisions here are highly personal, but here are some of the questions to ask yourself:

• Is the child's other parent Wiccan? If not, the two of you may face a difficult process of finding a fair and beneficial solution for your children.

• When your kid stands up in first grade and says "I'm Wiccan!", what's going to happen? In inhospitable areas, child-service investigators get called in; even in tolerant areas, the other kids may be reluctant to accept a child who isn't like them.

• If you're part of a Wiccan coven or study group, does the group welcome children? What arrangement is there for child care during rituals and planning sessions? If there is no arrangement, are you willing to start one? And are you willing to do your share, whether it be giving up your own ritual time to take a turn at child care or contributing money toward a sitter?

• Do you want to make a religious choice for your child? Most Wiccans come to their religion in early adulthood, specifically reject-ing the faith their parents chose for them. Some choose not to raise their own children as Wiccans, instead introducing them to many traditions and letting them make their own choices.

There are some parents who, considering all these factors, will confidently go on to raise their children as open Wiccans. Others will keep their religion quiet, practicing it as an adult activity and discussing it when the kids are old enough to understand the need for discretion. A few, in particularly difficult circumstances, may need to keep their religion secret from their own children. None of these choices is wrong.

No matter what faith your children are taught, you can teach them about the cycles of the natural world. Let them learn that we need rain as well as sun, dark as well as light, winter as well as summer. Help them understand the special environment of their hometown. What sorts of grasses grow there? What geological forces shaped this place? Where does your water come from? You may not know, but you and your kids can find out.

You can also teach them, through your actions as well as your words, about the value of truth and honor. Let them know that there is no dishonor in speaking one's own truth and braving the disap-proval of others. As they grow, let them know that your love will not keep them from the consequences of their actions.

Parents in Celtic mythology, like real parents, differ widely—some noble, some irresponsible. Motherhood in particular was considered a divine attribute, and three mothers (*Matronae* or *Matres*) are often revered together. In history, the Celtic queen Boudicca became a warrior after her daughters were raped. In later legends, Celtic mothers could and did take political and military action on behalf of their children.

The upbringing of children was hardly an all-female preserve. Few heroes of Celtic mythology reach maturity without help from a father, foster-father, or uncle (often one who conveniently happens to be a god or magician). The role of the father is sanctified in the Irish god Dagda, a powerful god of fertility whose offspring are said to include the goddess Brigid. He has both great wisdom and uncouth manners, providing for his divine family with an inexhaustible cauldron of food. Any parent struggling to provide for a family may find support and guidance in worshiping him.

The Celtic tradition of "fosterage" allowed families to cement political or economic ties by sending a child to be brought up in another household. In the Welsh and Irish legends, it is often a foster parent or uncle who is instrumental in bringing a child out of youth into adulthood. This tradition, and the obligations attached to it, may be of special significance to those who find themselves raising another's child or forced to live far away from their offspring. Another modern expression of fosterage might be to make sure your children have trusted adult friends, extra role models, and sources of support as they grow up.

Guardian Amulet for a Child

Parents throughout time have sought the help of the goddesses and gods in protecting their children. If your child is old enough to work with clay, he or she can help you craft a guardian amulet. With a baby or toddler, you can put your own energy into guarding the child's safety. This rite draws on the potent symbolism of the human head in Celtic art. In warrior tribes this was the severed head of an enemy; in more peaceful times and places, the protective heads belonged to gods and goddesses.

Choose a deity of guardianship. Of course, if your child has shown an interest in Celtic myths, this should be the god or goddess to whom the child feels closest. If no such attachment exists, I might invoke Macha, a powerful warrior goddess of Irish legend. In fact, there were three Machas. One was gifted with foresight, and warned of danger. One was gifted with power of war and sovereignty, and ruled Ireland. The third was gifted with physical strength and speed, and with magical abilities capable of striking back at the men who required her to run a race while heavily pregnant. She is an appropriate goddess to invoke when you are protecting that which means the most to you, for she is a land goddess first, and a war goddess only when that land is threatened. The rite below assumes you are working with Macha, but may of course be adapted to suit your own choice.

If your child is to be the artist, the two of you can talk about myths associated with the god or goddess you chose. Explain the purpose of the work, perhaps something like this: "I know that you're growing up and becoming more independent, and I won't be able to watch over you all the time, the way I did when you were a baby. Instead, we can do a piece of magic that will ask the goddess Macha to watch over you as you explore more of the world."

You'll need some polymer clay, which can be baked in the oven to harden, and some paints if desired. Find a place and time suitable for making a mess, and put on some music that makes you feel creative. Sit quietly for a few minutes before starting, then invoke Macha.

> *Prophet, warrior, ancient queen*
> *Honored one, I ask protection.*
> *Guard this child, still new and green*
> *In every place, time, and direction.*

In the clay, create your image of the head and face of Macha. It doesn't matter if the artwork is crude and childlike. In depicting sacred beings, intent was (and is) far more important than realism.

Make sure the head is small enough to be worn or carried on the body. If it is to be a pendant, make sure there's a hole or loop at the top. Do your work well, but do not linger when the inspiration and energy have faded. Bake as directed and make a gift of it to your child with these words:

> You are a child of the green earth
> And Macha will protect you.

If you wish to make a thanks-offering to Macha, visit a place where horses are kept and (after asking permission) feed the horses apples or carrots. More imaginatively, acts of kindness and hospitality toward pregnant women or nursing mothers can also be seen as honoring Macha. When the child reaches puberty, give him or her the option of offering the amulet itself to the goddess in thanks for her protection.

Home Life

Sometimes, home can be the hardest place to manifest Celtic Wiccan values. Yet if we are truly practicing our faith and not just celebrating holidays, we owe it to ourselves to become the heroes of our own legends, to strive within our own tribes to manifest the qualities we hold dear.

I said "strive." Don't expect perfection of yourself or anyone else. Those who know me will tell you that I am far from achieving all of these goals in my own home life. And in the legends, you'll find that even the gods make mistakes.

In "The Colloquy of the Ancients," a poem written in Christian Ireland but describing the nation's Pagan past, St. Patrick asks the ghost of the hero Caeilte what sustained the Fianna war-bands before the arrival of Christianity. Caeilte replies, "Truth that was in our hearts, and strength in our arms, and fulfillment in our tongues." These three—truth, strength and honor—may be said to represent a Celtic ideal.

Truth. This doesn't mean speaking out with complete honesty all the time, a practice guaranteed to cause trouble in home life. The people around you do not want to hear that their hair looks lousy or their cooking stinks. Manifesting this virtue means telling *yourself* the truth about the reasons for your actions. Are you making sacrifices for your partner because you want to, or because you feel you ought to? Do you want a tattoo as a symbol of your innermost self, or to irritate your parents? Are you yelling at your dog because you think that will teach it how to behave, or because you had a bad day?

If you've been living on the surface up till now, learning to explore your own motives can be difficult work. It requires challenging yourself and learning more about how your words and actions affect the world around you. And it means telling the truth to others when it's appropriate.

Writer Erynn Rowan Laurie says the ultimate value of truth for Celts was in making wise judgments, and this insight provides a useful rule of thumb. If withholding the truth will cause someone to make false judgments, then you must tell it. Telling someone "that outfit looks great" is usually an acceptable falsehood—but what if that person is on the way to a job interview and will suffer by not looking his or her best?

Strength. The Celts greatly valued physical valor and accomplishment, coupled with emotional resilience, culture, and bravery, and celebrated those qualities in both men and women.

Striving for physical health is the part that gives me the most trouble. Even a modest diet and exercise regimen is a challenge for someone addicted to the sedentary pursuits of the computer and the bookshelf! Pledging myself before the goddesses and gods to follow a path of health helps me to remember my intentions.

And of course, strength is not just physical. In daily travels, you use your strength to remain polite when the drivers around you are rude; to respect your friends even when they irritate you; to stand up for your rights when a store sells you inferior merchandise; to speak and act on behalf of political and charitable causes that are in keeping with your values. Your own life will present you with the challenges that will help you grow stronger. Understand and learn from those challenges.

Honor. In the eighth-century laws of Ireland, honor was literally worth money. A person's status in society dictated his or her "honor price," which had to be paid to the family or tribe if that person were killed. We have a different system for dealing with murders, but honor is no less important a concept. You earn it through noble and brave actions on behalf of your tribe (family). This doesn't mean seeking violent revenge on the officer who gave your sister a ticket. It means living in such a way as to protect and enhance your family's well-being—everything from conserving money to being polite to the neighbors. It means standing with your family and defending its interests, even on those days when you're tempted to claim you're an orphan.

Worshiping in a study group or coven often has the effect of turning the group into a second family. For many Celtic Wiccans, this is an empowering moment—the chance to choose one's own tribe. Not every tribe is right for every person, so please examine the group carefully before taking on obligations that will bind you in honor. If they are careful of their own honor, they will subject you to the same scrutiny.

As my commitment to my faith has grown, I've changed some of my choices because I've started to see myself as a representative of my religion. I have become more responsible, striving to treat others in a way that increases the honor of my people. Many people who know me don't know my faith; I aspire to live so that if they find out, they will think better of this religion.

A Spell for Harmony in the Home

I've written a lot about the responsibilities we have at home, because they're important and because we can't truly change anyone but ourselves. Still, if you're trying to do all this work in a difficult environment, it's hard to bring energy and concentration to your daily round. So this is a spell to create a little space of renewal and good humor in your room, apartment, or house, a recharging station in which you can repair your energy and process the events of the day.

Depending on your circumstances, you may wish to invite those who share your living space to take part in this rite, and older children may enjoy taking a role. This spell is also entirely suited for solitary practice. First, you'll need to assemble a few things: lavender incense, a bowl of water, a bowl of salt, and a broom.

If others are participating, you can divide the roles among up to five participants: the ritual leader (you), the Banisher, and the invokers of Land, Sea, and Sky. Create a thoughtful atmosphere by putting on some quiet New Age, Celtic, or classical music; if possible dim the lights and add some candlelight.

Gather the participants at the northernmost part of the space to be protected. Leave the closest door or window slightly open. Ask everyone to stand for a few minutes to concentrate. In your mind or out loud, call on the goddess or god to whom you feel the strongest connection, and ask for blessings and harmony for your home. I might choose Epona, whose attributes include protection of domestic resources, or Nantosuelta, who is associated with the household and with the underworld.

When you are ready to begin, nod to the Banisher, who steps forward to the northernmost point, holds up the broom and chants:

> By the moon and by the sun
> Let all that would do harm be gone,
> By the stars and by the tide
> Let only harmony abide.

The Banisher travels around the inner perimeter of the house counterclockwise (to the left, or "widdershins"), making sweeping motions with the broom. The other participants follow. At the end of this journey, the Banisher makes a strong sweeping motion toward the open door or window, sending all negative energy out of the house, then closes the door or window and says.

> By earth, by wind, by flame, by sea
> As I will, so shall it be!

Other participants repeat this couplet (and do so again each time it is spoken).

Next, the Land invoker holds up the bowl of salt and says:

> *Powers of the Sacred Land*
> *Uphold the home in which we stand.*

That person then takes a tiny pinch of the salt between two fingers and rubs them together, causing particles of salt to drop to the ground, and chants *"By earth, by wind . . ."*

The Water invoker steps up next, and holds up the bowl of water and says:

> *Powers of the Resounding Sea*
> *Surround this place with harmony.*

Then that person dips his or her fingers into the water and allows a drop or two to fall to the floor. Again the chant: *"By earth, by wind . . ."*

The Sky invoker lights the incense. (If someone in your household has a reaction to incense, you can substitute lavender flowers or a candle anointed with non-chemical lavender oil.)

> *Powers of the Radiant Skies*
> *Let love and wisdom be our prize.*

The Sky invoker closes with *"By earth, by wind . . ."* echoed by other participants.

Now each of you commits to doing your share toward preserving the atmosphere you've created. As ritual leader, you go first. Step forward and face either the north (if working alone) or the others in your household. The oath follows a formula from the Irish myths:

> *I swear,*
> *By the gods my people swear by,*
> *To uphold the harmony of this home.*

Other participants repeat the oath, but may substitute their own gods or guiding principles.

When you are done, thank the gods and the people of your

household. Leave the incense burning for a time to let the energy flow through the space.

Take Pleasure

By some modern standards, members of Celtic tribes had it rough in daily life, and certainly they had to work harder than we do for such comforts as heating and water. Yet they found great joy in life, and the tales about them describe their love for feasting, poetry, music, and other pleasures.

If you find the daily grind wearing away at your spirit, make an effort to clear away influences that drain you or throw your life off balance. Seek the company of positive, energizing people. Spend time appreciating the gifts of nature. Pause to enjoy the blessings the gods give us. Find pleasure in learning and creativity, in doing your duty with honor, and in making your world a better place. Renew yourself through art and worship, and use the resulting energy to make positive changes for yourself.

In seeking balance and honor in my own life, I've found that living my beliefs is not a burdensome chore, but a source of renewal, accomplishment, and joy.

SEVEN

Seasonal Rituals

The evidence we have gives hints as to what events the Celts might have honored with a festival or ritual: the beginning or end of a battle, the start of work on a temple, tomb, or other large community building, the death of a leader. Virtually every religion has seasonal festivals of some kind. Marking the cycles of dark and light, cold and warmth, growth and death seems to be a basic human need. Though no evidence of a "Celtic ritual year" can be said to truly exist, we know of four seasonal festivals celebrated in at least some Celtic areas.

Out of respect for the cycles of nature (and perhaps because they like parties), Wiccans have added the solstices and equinoxes to these to form a "Wheel of the Year" of eight festivals. Learned Celts knew of these solar dates, certainly. The Coligny Calendar (a sophisticated reckoning of the year, written in Latin but using Celtic concepts) indicates a high level of astronomical knowledge. In addition, new evidence from soil sampling and sophisticated archaeological analysis is revealing that the Celts were knowledgeable and successful farmers, who would necessarily be deeply aware of the cycles of light and dark.

Interestingly, Julius Caesar writes that the Celts divided time by nights rather than by days—that is, what we call Tuesday evening would in their system have been part of Wednesday. This ties in with fragmentary evidence that may indicate the Celtic year began and ended at the beginning of winter, with the dark time counted as part of a unit with the light that followed.

Most Wiccans commemorate all eight of these days in this "Wheel of the Year" in some form. For the sake of convenience, it is often necessary to celebrate on a day near, rather than on, the "official" date. In some cases, the astronomical date of the solstice or equinox may be a day before or after the date I've given. The timing of your celebrations will depend on your own inclinations, the community available to you, and the circumstances of your life.

For some, the Great Days (as many Wiccans call them) are times for deep, personal rituals of exploration and growth, done alone or with a small coven. For many, though, these days are times to gather in groups, see old friends and make new ones, and perform rituals of community and celebration. In this chapter, I'll offer ideas for both forms of ritual, as well as a brief sketch of historical customs when they are known.

This chapter will not set out full-text rituals, instead inviting you to use your creativity toward constructing your own. The seasons and solar days are described here as they appear to a European or North American. Wiccans who dwell in the Southern Hemisphere will naturally reverse them, and will no doubt apply their own creative energy to rituals that make sense within their cycle of seasons.

Yule, or Winter Solstice (December 21)

History: At one time, we know, the solstices and equinoxes were important to the people dwelling in Great Britain, for they built great structures oriented toward the sun's light on those special days. However, not all their structures were so oriented, and archaeologists have been unable to establish the purpose of these observations or the significance the days might have had in these societies. In any case, these structures were built centuries before the coming of the people we can identify today as Celts.

For warriors, merchants, and rulers, this may have been a relatively restful time, with the season of military campaigning over, the weather preventing long journeys for trading. In winter quarters, we can imagine artisans repairing armor and weapons, musicians and poets entertaining the rulers, and perhaps internal power struggles as the tribe worked to position itself for the next year's efforts. Hunting helped extend the food supply and vary the diet, and also provided a way to work off fighters' energy and keep their skills honed.

For farmers, this was a critical time. Having done everything possible to assure sufficient food for the winter, they turned to the woods, both for fuel and to harvest timber for building projects. Peter J. Reynolds, director of a British model farm created to test ancient techniques, writes of the importance of laying in sufficient firewood to cure for one or two years, along with "working wood" for everything from chariots to dishes to farm implements. Yule logs and Christmas trees, both drawn from later Germanic cultures, may reflect traditions associated with this part of the working year.

This season is of course associated with Christmas in Western culture, and many Wiccans follow the traditions of their youth by devoting their greatest energies to this festival. Customs borrowed from many sources (including other ancient Pagan cultures) make up the modern Wiccan celebration, including Yule logs, decorated trees, bright lights, and the exchange of gifts. In addition, many Wiccans celebrate Christmas, Hanukkah, or Kwanzaa with their non-Pagan friends or families. There is nothing wrong with doing this, even if it means going to a service for a religion that isn't your own. The important thing is to use this time in celebrations that will sustain your spirit through the winter weeks ahead.

In Solitary Practice: Going to parties, putting on rituals, buying and wrapping gifts, decorating one's home, visiting family, and cooking holiday food are all delightful things to do. But if you try to do them all, and please too many people, it's easy to become anxious and unhappy. Taking some quiet time at this season is a precious gift you can give yourself.

Give yourself permission to set the bustle aside for a few hours. Find a time and place to experience the beauty of the winter, perhaps more muted than that of other seasons, but natural and refreshing nonetheless. For centuries people have found solace in turning dark into light with candles and lamps. Decorating your home or altar with holiday lights is entirely appropriate, as is candle meditation.

This is a time of renewal and faith. The dark always *does* get shorter, the light always *does* get longer. Yet at the depth of the winter, when work or school may keep you from seeing the sun at all, when the land is gray and bleak, it may be tough to remember this. Seasonal rites of this time are geared toward reminding ourselves (and asking for divine reassurance) that the snow will melt, that the light will return, that the land will turn green and fruitful once more. Ultimately, the faith that gets us through the dark of winter reminds us that renewal and rebirth are possible within ourselves as well.

At this busy season, make sure you put your energy into those people, traditions, and activities that mean the most to you. If you can, give some time and resources to someone in need, whether that need be physical, emotional, or spiritual. Take time to be with the people who make you feel most positive, and use your time alone to help you stay focused on enjoying rather than enduring the season.

Suggestion: Set aside a single evening during the crowded holiday season to be alone in worship. Light a candle or lamp, and cast a circle in which to meditate. Offer thanks to a chosen god or goddess for all the blessings you enjoy at this season. Ask for renewal and rebirth in those areas of your life that require it. If you have a personal symbol of sun and summer, particularly if made by your own hands, set it up on your altar, or consider making it an offering of art to the gods, to bring the light and warmth back. Most of all, though, spend this entire evening resting and relaxing, doing not what will please others, but whatever will renew and inspire you with the spirit of the season.

In Group Worship: At this time of the year, ancient tribes found the land no longer fruitful, and relied for food on their stores and their hunting skills. Build up the stores of your "tribe" (the larger community where you live) by developing a Pagan public-service project to help those less fortunate than you. Collecting food, clothing, or money may not seem like a form of worship, but it is. You might even hold a brief ritual to bless your gleanings before giving them away.

Some Pagan groups participate in multifaith events such as educational displays, musical events, and even classroom presentations. If handled with grace, these efforts can be a valuable way to introduce your community to the Pagans who dwell within it. This is also an auspicious time for marriages and handfastings, and many couples enjoy starting off their unions on the longest night of the year!

In keeping with seasonal customs in the wider culture, many groups put on feasts, dedicating their culinary efforts to the gods and goddesses of their worship. Other Wiccan solstice customs include gift exchanges with a decorated "Yule tree" and adorning homes with evergreen boughs and lights. Rituals at this time tend to be lively and festive. Many groups raise energy to "turn the wheel" or "bring back the light." This can be a delightful, kid-friendly type of ritual, making lots of noise with voices, drums, and whatever else you have.

Suggestion: Design a ritual honoring Epona, the Celtic horse goddess, whose festival was December 18. As a guardian of domestic life, Epona is particularly suited for family worship, and young children can invoke her through drawings, poems, songs, and pretend-play that relates to horses. Ask her protection for your home and all that you hold dear. Epona is also associated with travel and journeys, and is a suitable deity to invoke for those who journey on land or in spirit. At a recent solstice ritual at my house, each participant took home a small metal horse charm, strung on a black cord, so that it could be worn about the neck or draped over a rear-view mirror.

Imbolc (February 1)

History: Though this holiday became part of the Christian calendar, first as St. Brigid's Day and then as Candlemas (February 2), it is still possible to discern some thread of ancient worship from the tales that remain about St. Brigid. The name of this holiday (also called Oimelc) first appears in the writings of the early Irish monks, and may be derived from words describing the coming of the ewes' milk, an early sign of the returning spring in an agricultural society.

In addition, agricultural communities may have harvested reeds during the winter, using the harsh season to improve the thatching on their rooftops and the insulation on their houses. Interestingly, the "Brigid's cross," a simple four-armed woven decoration associated with St. Brigid in later Irish folk custom, is also traditionally made of reeds.

As discussed in the Gods and Goddesses chapter, Brigid was probably a real fifth-century woman, but her name and the qualities associated with her quite possibly tap into something Pagan. At this season it was apparently customary to light bonfires on hilltops, and offer prayers for the fertility of the tribe (including crops, livestock, and humans).

In Solitary Worship: While this time of year brings forbidding weather in most climates, the cold and snow often make it possible to do outdoor rituals without fear of interruption. An outdoor rite in northern climates should probably be brief, and include lots of invigorating walking to keep you warm! If you live near a river or other body of water, make an offering of milk or bread to Brigid there. At this season, take note of the first signs of returning growth. Even if the ground is thick with snow—as it often is at my house on Imbolc—meditate on the life that begins to stir beneath the ground.

Indoors, use this season to think about your creative life. Does it need renewing? This may be the time to resume work on an old project or take up a new creative path. Make an offering of art to Brigid in her aspect as patroness of poets.

Also, assess your own physical and mental health. Brigid the healer will help you in your efforts to heal yourself, but you should also seek the help of trained healers for whatever needs attention (don't forget your eyes and teeth!). Offer a quick prayer to Brigid before you begin a physical workout, asking her blessings of health and strength. If you feel good when you are through exercising, offer thanks, both to strengthen your connection with the goddess and to imprint that good feeling on your mind, so that you are motivated to stay active.

If you have been thinking of learning a form of healing—anything from medical school to massage—now is a good time to begin. Ask Brigid's blessing upon the seeds of healing herbs, then plant them in pots.

As at Yule, candles and lamps are appropriate, but so are larger fires. If you have access to a fireplace, fire pit, or other place to safely build a fire, do so, and offer incense to the flames in Brigid's name. On a more practical note, Brigid also protects against fire and lightning. Use her holiday as a reminder to check the fire-protection systems in your home, hold fire-safety drills with your family, and ask her aid in keeping your home safe.

Suggestion: Create a Brigid altar, with your own handmade image of the goddess. Use incense or scented oils that remind you of healing (perhaps lavender, lilac, or rosemary). On Imbolc night, place a small bowl of milk on the altar in offering, and light a candle. Ask Brigid to inspire you with good health, skillful hands, and a creative spirit. Remain in meditation, and be open to ideas that come to you during this time, which may be Brigid's way of showing you how to achieve these goals. When you are through, the milk may be poured outdoors.

In Group Worship: I once belonged to a coven that insisted on an outdoor bonfire every Imbolc. We few would tramp through the frigid woods, sliding on the ice and snow, and hastily build and light the fire. The ritual at the bonfire was indeed magical, and it was easy to understand the allure of this rite in the days before electric lighting and central heat. For a group of relatively healthy people, this is a wonderful way to celebrate the season, and I recommend it highly.

If you are indoors, consider ways of making a symbolic bonfire. This can be as simple as a small candle or lamp, or could be more dramatic. Some will hold their rituals around a fireplace, or place a small amount of alcohol in a metal bowl and burn it off.

This is a good time for a group to work on a creative project together, do healing rituals, or bless new magical tools. Raise energy to awaken the new life that lies beneath the ground, and realize that each of us has growth and power within us, gathering strength.

Suggestion: Light a fire or large candle at the center of your circle. Give each participant a small votive candle and go around the circle, each person lighting his or her candle and telling a brief story of healing or transformation, or reading a poem. As each person takes his or turn, watch as your circle becomes a magical place of light!

Spring Equinox (March 21)

History: In his book *Stations of the Sun*, which traces the history of current British holiday celebrations, historian Ronald Hutton points out that the Spring Equinox is not a likely time to celebrate the beginning of spring in most of Britain. There, the ground is already green and blooming in March. In North America, however, spring tends to come later, and the equinox provides the first festival of the season. Whether the land in your area is in full flower or just emerging from winter into "mud season," the equinox is a time of thanks and celebration of new life, with the sun's returning light and warmth.

For the Celts, it was also a time of hard work. Those who made their way by warfare and raiding began their season of campaigning when the ground was dry, and thus this may have been a time of preparation and scouting potential enemies. Farmers, carefully watching the weather and relying on past seasons' experience, hitched their cattle to their plows and took to the fields to break up the winter soil.

The Celts are credited with inventing the iron plowshare, really an iron sheath that fitted over part of a sophisticated wooden plow to prevent wear. Scientific evidence suggests that Celtic farmers of the third through first centuries B.C.E. cross-plowed their fields— that is, they went over every piece of ground twice, in different directions, to further loosen the soil. Reynolds speculates that a typical farmer may have spent two solid weeks on this work, then another week on planting. Crops may have included grains, vegetables and even flax (useful for oil as well as linen).

Besides the sheer labor, this time of year also required tricky calculations of when to start and what to plant where and when, so as to get the most for the farmers' toil. They most likely understood crop rotation and may even have mixed crops in the same field— wheat and beans, for example. Even with modern agricultural chemicals and technology, each spring is a gamble. It is easy to imagine that the Celts sought help from their gods at this time.

In the Christian calendar the equinox heralds the coming of Easter, the festival of resurrection. The name "Easter" is widely presumed to come from the name of a Germanic goddess, but may in fact simply come from a word-root meaning "dawn" or "beginning." In any case, the return of spring has always been a compelling reason for celebration.

In Solitary Worship: One of the natural tokens of spring is the rush of flowing water in lakes, rivers, and streams. The ice and snow that fell from Yule through Imbolc finally melts, and whether the nearest ice is outside your door or far off in the mountains, the effect is the same. We know that water was important to the Celts, and on this holiday we can offer our thanks for clean, flowing water.

Water is a potent purifier, and rituals at this time might involve using water to do some magical "spring cleaning." While you're at it, go through some of your household stuff and give away what you no longer use. Use the new light to really clean the place where you live. Then mix water with a small amount of aromatic oil (a floral scent might be most appropriate) and scatter drops around your environment. For self-cleansing, make a ritual bath with cleansing herbs (herbalist and magician Paul Beyerl lists basil and hyssop as possibilities) and wash yourself with the strong intention to rid yourself of whatever is holding you back from participating in the renewal of yourself and your life.

Equinoxes are also times of balance, when the light and the dark are equal in time. This is a good time to examine the balance of your own life. Is there any area of life in which you are doing too much, or not enough? This is not a process meant to induce guilt, but simply acceptance, acknowledgment, and the conscious decision to bring your life back into equilibrium.

Suggestion: Go to a beach, lake, stream, or river. If you are sure it is safe to drink this water, gather some on the spot; otherwise, bring a container of fresh water with you. Set up a circle and invoke a god or goddess of water, or one with whom you have a special connection. Wet your fingers with the water and touch them to your heart, asking that your emotions be cleansed and ready to accept new life. Do the same thing with your "third eye" (the center of your forehead), asking that your mind be cleansed and ready to accept new wisdom. Finally, touch a few drops of water to each eyelid, asking that your sight be cleansed and ready to accept new light. Offer the rest of the water to the earth.

In Group Worship: In northern places, such as the one where I live, late March is often a time of unpredictable weather. By all means plan an outdoor ritual, but have a backup plan. Many years ago I was one of a group who made plans to get up early and celebrate the equinox at sunrise on a distant beach, only to discover that nine inches of snow had fallen while we slept, and we couldn't even get out of the driveway! Weather permitting, you may wish to greet the sunrise (like springtime, a symbol of new light and life). Consider organizing some project to care for the land in your area, such as maintaining trails at a park or planting trees on land you own.

Many Wiccan groups use this ritual to bless seeds for the spring planting, and this is entirely appropriate even if your "farm" is a few pots by a window. In some cases, it may be possible to bless herb seeds that participants then plant during the ritual, perhaps associating the planting with initiatives they want to take in their own lives. Taking this a step further, one might plan a ritual with a plowing theme, with participants breaking up a symbolic amount of soil with their hands as a way of breaking through anything that is holding them back from their full potential for growth. Finally, consider arranging a group project to plant flowers at a traffic island or in another public place.

Suggestion: In many areas, spring brings a return of the chorus of birdsong. Birds were important in Celtic art and later Irish and Welsh mythology, and were associated with everything from war to prophecy. To honor the birds and your chosen deity, create a ritual of song, in which music takes a central role. If you have experienced musicians in your group, so much the better, but if you don't, just take a few simple songs or chants and practice them until you feel comfortable singing them. Many Wiccans have brought music into their rituals by writing suitable words to tunes that everyone knows (a technique dating back to medieval times). Your performance needn't be perfect—just give the best music you've got to give. Along with this, try a guided meditation in which participants experience flying, seeing the newly green earth below them.

Beltane (May 1)

History: The Irish *Cormac's Glossary*, written in about 900 C.E., can be seen as indicating some practices that survived in Ireland from before Christianity. One of them, the custom of a festival at the beginning of May, was called Beltane, or "lucky fire." The custom that inspired it was agricultural—the celebrants built two fires, then drove the cows between the two to bless the herd with luck on its way to summer pastures. We can't know precisely how old the practice is, but we do know that related folk customs survived well into the nineteenth century.

Along with moving livestock to summer grazing areas, farm families hoed crops and supervised births of their animals' young. They no doubt welcomed the fresh greens and berries that became available at this time. For the first time since fall, it was possible to travel on roads unimpeded by snow or mud, and this may have been a popular time for trading.

Today, the advent of truly warm weather, the pleasantness of the sky and land and air in May, and the natural inclinations of humans have made this more than a mere farmers' festival. Lacking details of ancient festivities, modern Wicca has drawn on folk customs of the past millennium to craft celebrations that include joy and thanks for the fertility of the earth and its people. Fresh flowers, seeds, and foodstuffs are part of the ritual, which often takes place outdoors. In many cases, Beltane rituals have a specific element of courtship and sexuality, and whether for this or other reasons, this is a favorite celebration for many.

In Solitary Worship: A suitable rite for this time of year might be as simple as looking at the sky and the trees and the grass and offering a heartfelt "Thank you!"

If you are in a relationship, this may be a time to do a ritual with your partner to renew the life and pleasure in your union. This is specifically an excellent time to do ritual workings toward conceiving a child (so if you don't want to do this, use extra care!). The magic of a loving partnership is not to be underestimated, and can be directed toward any goal you share.

If you do not have a partner, and would like one, this may be a good time to do love magic. The Romans believed May to be an unlucky time for marriage (which is where we get the custom of marrying in June), but in some parts of early Christian Ireland, trial marriages were begun at Beltane. In these, the partners agreed to stay together for a "year and a day" before permanently sealing the match or going their separate ways.

Suggestion: In a Welsh story from the *Mabinogion*, a collection first published in the mid-thirteenth century, the magician Math helps Llew (a many-skilled young man, probably akin to the Irish god

Lugh) defy a curse. Among the taboos placed on Llew by his mother Arianrhod is that he will never have a human wife. Math instead fashions a woman out of flowers, brings her to life by his magic, and gives the lady Blodeuwedd to Llew as wife.

While the marriage turned out rather badly (the lady fell in love with someone else), the ritual itself was a success. A solitary Beltane rite might include an adaptation of Math's technique. Obtain some long-stemmed flowers and tie them together into a roughly human shape. Place this on your altar, either inside or in a place of nature. Cast your circle and light two candles in the center, a couple of feet apart so that you have room to walk between them. Holding your flower-person, invoke a deity you associate with love (perhaps Rosmerta, either with or without her Roman partner Mercury) and ask for help in opening yourself to a new love. Be very careful not to associate any particular person with this prayer, for to do so would be a violation of that person's freedom. Then, still holding the flowers, walk between the two candles, knowing that this is a magical gateway on this Beltane night. Leave the flowers in a place of nature. When you are happily partnered, return to that place and make a thanks-offering.

In Group Worship: Many groups choose a man and woman to be King and Queen of the May. Sometimes these are chosen by lot, with the resulting entertainment and embarrassment for the pair of being coupled in everyone's eyes. More often, the roles go to an existing couple (who need not be of opposite genders). If your group does this, try to choose the couple whose attitudes toward each other best reflect joy and love.

The King and Queen then preside over a ritual and feast, in which flowers and greenery predominate. A bonfire is traditional, and as it dies down, participants jump the fire for luck. Flowers are a customary part of the ritual, and the branch of a flowering tree (taken carefully, with respect for the tree) is a particularly potent symbol of the new season.

Following British folk customs, some groups do a form of lot-drawing, sometimes called "bannock" after a Scottish bread used in this rite. In its simplest form, one piece of the bread is marked with charcoal, and the person who gets that piece must perform some purifying ritual such as jumping the fire seven times. In a more complex version, small tokens (today, wrapped in foil for the sake of hygiene) are placed in the bread before it is baked, and the one you get signifies your luck for the year. The tokens and meanings vary, but this set will work: a penny means money, a stick means poverty, a ring means love, and a needle means hard work.

Suggestion: Maypoles, which began as a medieval English custom, have been variously connected with sexual and religious imagery, but may just be a spontaneous celebration of the splendor of nature at this time of year. For this ritual, try to gather a larger group, perhaps including those who might not have seen each other during the winter. Consider working with other groups in your area, or holding a large open festival.

For this, you'll need a large straight pole, preferably a tree trunk of reasonable size. You'll also need an outdoor ritual site where it's OK to dig a hole in the ground. Most public parks frown on this, because holes in a lawn are hard to repair. A tradition among Wiccans in my area is to hold the festival at a beach, so that we can fill the hole in the sand back in when we're done, with no harm to the place. Some groups use the same maypole each year. Others favor an alternate form of recycling: The Yule tree becomes the maypole, and the maypole becomes the following year's Yule log.

Cut off the branches, so that you have a long pole. Some prefer to remove the bark, then sand and paint the trunk; others simply decorate the pole with colorful garlands. On the day of the ritual, convey this pole to an outdoor spot. Make an occasion of carrying it to the ritual site, with songs and chants to welcome the May. Dig a hole of sufficient depth to provide a firm foundation, and lay the pole next to it. In keeping with the Celtic custom of making offerings in pits, you might place flowers, pennies, or other objects in the bottom of the hole for luck.

Choose two or three people to raise the maypole, and have the rest form a circle to sing or perhaps do a simple circle dance as it goes up. You can adorn it with ribbons and flowers, and make it the central point of your ritual, perhaps symbolizing a tree-god. Many groups regard the placing of the pole in the earth as a symbolic sexual rite, invoking the fertility of the earth.

For a more ambitious ritual, have each person bring several feet of ribbon (twice the length of the pole, perhaps) and fasten each ribbon securely to the top of the pole before it is raised. Then you're set for a maypole dance! Everyone stands in a circle around the pole, holding his or her ribbon. Ideally, the circle should alternate between men and women, but this isn't often possible or practical. What's important is that every second person around the circle should turn to the left, and the remaining people to the right, so that they're facing one another. The dance goes like this: Step to your right as you go forward to pass the person in front of you. Then step to your left to go around and pass the next person, and back to the right for the person after that. If you can't have a drummer, musician, or stereo outside the circle, try a very simple chant, but don't make things too complex for the dancers!

Once you get going, the group's ribbons will begin to weave into a pattern around the pole, and the circles will get smaller and closer as your ribbons get shorter. See how this dance came to be associated with flirting? When the dance is done, leave the pole up, with ribbons flying, while the group enjoys a picnic feast.

As you leave the ritual site, participants may carry the decorated pole between two fires or torches for luck.

Summer Solstice (June 21)

History: This time of the longest light is a time of fruitfulness and pageantry, a time to honor the glories of the sun and the bounty of the earth. More practically, it is another natural break in the agricultural year, just before the haying season begins. For warriors, this was prime campaigning season, and the artisans and Druids were perhaps materially and spiritually keeping the fighters well-equipped.

We have one fourth-century mention, by a Christian saint, of a

Pagan custom that may be associated with this day: Villagers built a wooden wheel (a solar symbol), set it on fire, and rolled it down a hill to a river, then took the charred pieces and offered them in the temple of a sky god.

We don't know much about the Celtic sun- or sky-god, for during the Romano-Celtic period his imagery was blended thoroughly with that of the Roman Jupiter. We know this god existed, though. On the Gundestrup Cauldron, he is pictured receiving an offering of a sun-wheel from a horned attendant, and the sun-wheel symbol is a common one in Celtic art. As the Romans introduced and spread the concept of representing gods directly in art, depictions of this god become more common, but they also reflect more and more of the associations of Jupiter.

We do not know what the sun-god was called in Britain, so for the sake of convenience we will borrow a name from the Celtic tribes of Austria and call him Belenus. (Many books confidently link this name with the British sun-god, and go on to establish Beltane as his celebration. There is only fragmentary evidence that this name made it to Britain, and the word root of "bel-" simply means "bright," so it's natural that it would occur in many contexts. But we'll use his name here anyway, recognizing that it may not be what he was called in ancient times.)

In Solitary Worship: Create a personal feast based on locally grown fresh produce, and eat it in your circle or outdoors, offering some to Belenus in thanks for the bounty of the earth. This is also a good time to do rituals for protection from thunder and storms. In some areas, this celebration falls at the beginning of hurricane or tornado season, giving greater impetus to such protective workings.

At this time of greatest light, take time to enjoy the beauty of the sun, and to reflect on the plenty and light in your life. If things are going well, make a conscious acknowledgment of that fact, imprinting it on your memory. Use your creativity to create a personal symbol of light and warmth that you will take with you into the winter. Reflect on what you have learned and the ways you have grown since the last solstice. What would you like to do differently? What makes you proud of yourself?

This is an excellent time to learn more about the land around you. Take a nature hike at a local park or sanctuary, or consider a summer class in herbalism or ecology.

Suggestion: The Celtic sun-god is a warrior god, for ancient armies spent the warm months on campaign. Many of the ancient depictions of the Romano-Celtic "Jupiter" show him squashing a subservient enemy.

For most of us, the actuality of war is a distant thing. If you're in the military or in law enforcement, you may wish to invoke Belenus to protect and empower your service. As a personal and spiritual campaign, choose an area of life in which you wish to improve yourself. Perhaps you wish to fight against shyness, to control a fierce temper, or to do battle against your own fears. Whatever you select will be your enemy in this rite.

In your circle, surround yourself with solar symbols—yellow and orange candles, wheels, circles, gold-colored objects. Bring at least one daisy (a flower traditionally connected with the sun) to the circle, and place the flower on the altar along with a pendant or stone that symbolizes protection. If you are comfortable doing ritual in the nude ("skyclad") and can do so in privacy, consider disrobing as the Celtic warriors did.

A warrior needs three things: a weapon, some form of protection, and an enemy. In this ritual, the flowers will symbolize the enemy, the pendant or stone the shield. The weapon is yourself—your intelligence, courage, and skill, which Belenus can empower.

First, hold the flowers and speak to them, describing them as your enemy. (For instance: "You are my deepest fear, the fear of failure, the fear that stops me from doing my best under pressure.") Be as accurate and honest as you can in making this description, for part of a warrior's job is to accurately assess the situation and the enemy's strength.

Next invoke the god Belenus, seeing him perhaps as a bearded man wielding a sun-wheel, crushing an enemy beneath his foot. Make an offering to him (perhaps wine, or a solar herb such as mistletoe or lavender) and ask his blessing upon your battle, praying that your hand, heart, and mind be strengthened in your effort to become a better person.

Finally, hold your pendant or stone, and ask Belenus to bless it with his power and protection, that it may help keep your deepest self safe from harm in your inner struggle. Speak aloud to him any promise you wish to make to commit yourself to becoming a better person and defeating that which is holding you back. Still holding the stone, turn your attention to the flowers and proclaim to them that Belenus protects you. Add a symbolic act of destruction, such as laying the flowers down and hitting them with the stone or stomping on them as you banish the qualities they represent.

When you have bid Belenus a respectful farewell and ended your ritual, scatter the flowers purposefully in a place of nature, where the sun will shine on them and where their essence will be returned to the earth. Carry your stone or wear your pendant until the next Dark Moon, or until the Winter Solstice, whichever is more appropriate to the enemy you face.

This ritual will work best, of course, if you combine it with a program of doing practical work to confront your inner enemy and overcome its influence or turn its energy to productive purposes.

In Group Worship: The Summer Solstice is a beautiful time of year, yet the rites of this time are a little more solemn than at Beltane. Already it is time to begin looking toward the dark and the winter, planning to store up whatever reserves, physical or spiritual, you may need during that time.

Many couples choose to get married or handfasted at this time of greatest light. Whatever rite you're doing, plan a feast with fresh, in-season foods, and give thanks for the bounty received and that yet to come. It is not too late to ritually "plant" new seeds of intention for positive change.

One of the most powerful uses for the light, warmth, and energy of this time is healing. If one among you is in need of healing, the energy of a group can be a strong positive force for good. On a purely practical level, an ill person who has the support of friends or family, and a strong sustaining belief of some kind, is more likely to put the force of his or her own will toward becoming healthy. If no one is particularly ill, a preventative working, blessing each participant with the smoke of a healing incense or a touch of healing oil, may be a suitable way to use the energy of the season.

Suggestion: If your group is environmentally minded, choose a day near the solstice to organize a litter cleanup at a public park, beach, or even a cemetery. Start well in advance by contacting the agency responsible for your chosen place and making all the necessary arrangements. Obtain supplies such as trash bags and rubber gloves for all who plan to participate.

Before you start, gather together, ground and center, and spend a few moments in meditation, attuning yourself to the natural world around you. Even if you're in a city park, try to listen for birdsong and the sound of wind in trees. As you work, use songs or chants to keep focused. Depending on the type of place you're in, you may wish to invoke a goddess or god associated with similar places— Cernunnos for a forest, Sulis for a spring and so on. It is perfectly OK not to do this, and to simply make your work an offering to the spirit of the place (*genius loci*, the Romans called it).

When you are finished, pour some wine or juice on the ground, and leave some birdseed as a final gift. You may wish to enjoy your work by holding a picnic feast after the cleanup. If you plan to hold a formal ritual at this point, consider raising energy toward the healing of the natural world.

Lughnasadh (August 1)

History: This is one of the days for which we have a reasonably rich story, courtesy of the Irish mythologies, which describe the god Lugh inaugurating the festival, either to honor his foster mother Tailtiu or to celebrate his marriage.

This may have been a harvest celebration, perhaps originally held slightly later in the year. Celtic communities were exporting grain and other agricultural products well before the Romans invaded, and the prosperity evidenced in some of their grave goods may testify to the success of some of their endeavors. We also know that the Celts were agricultural innovators, inventing the iron-tipped plowshare and the first harvesting machine, which the Roman historian Strabo described as a cart pushed by an ox, with toothed wooden edges to strip ears of grain off their stalks. In any case, this would have been a time of long hours of hard work, and a break would have been more than welcome.

It was also a time when the land tended to be dry and the weather warm. In other words, it was (and is) a good time to hold regional festivals and market days, with people gathering from a distance to trade their wares, show off their skills, and kick up their heels.

The early-medieval Irish myths say Lughnasadh (pronounced "loo-NAH-sah") may have originated with funeral games, and indeed the day is still tinged with a darker side. Lugh's story ends in his death and betrayal, and the ancients may well have performed a sacrifice of some kind at the start of the harvest to ensure its successful completion. Such an act echoes the destruction of the grain itself, which must take place so that the harvested grain can sustain the lives of the people who grew it. This kind of sacrifice also has parallels in the later mythology, where one can trace a theme of "sacrificed kings" whose lives are given to benefit the people they rule.

In Solitary Worship: By now the days have grown noticeably shorter, and in ancient times a prudent community would have begun to see to its stores, putting food and fuel aside during the time of plenty so as to make it through the winter. While it may be burning hot outside, the cold *is* coming. Look around you: What have you begun to "harvest" from the efforts you began earlier this year? What more can you hope to achieve in the months ahead? Meditate on the nature of the work you must do to fully realize those hopes.

Lugh was above all a god of skill, and if you have been working to improve a skill, particularly in some creative path, now is an excellent time to make offerings of thanks. This is also a good time to consciously reflect on your skills and consider adding to them. Is there a class that could make you a better-paid employee? A new artistic path that could refresh and renew your mind? An unfinished degree waiting for you to revisit your studies? If you have been thinking of marketing your skills or selling the fruits of your art, now is a good time to start.

Suggestion: Choose a relatively cool time of day when you have access to a kitchen, perhaps late evening or early morning. Mix a batch of biscuit dough, following any standard recipe (you can even use a mix). Gather a flat pan and a few bottles of food coloring or some edible herbs you associate with prosperity or skill. Either in your sacred space or in the kitchen, open your ritual as you normally would, then invoke Lugh and ask his blessing upon your bread.

Mix the dough in a bowl till it forms a coherent whole, then put it onto the pan. Use your colors and herbs for decoration and flavoring. Knead with your hands (go on, get messy!) as you speak aloud the hopes you seek to harvest in the weeks ahead, and what you wish to have stored up in your mind and heart before winter sets in. Make a little chant or song of some of your words as you knead and shape the dough into a roughly human form. End this part of your ritual and set the bread to bake according to your recipe.

When the bread is done and cooled, take the head of the loaf outdoors and make it a sacrifice to nature by crumbling it up and scattering the crumbs for birds or other creatures. Eat at least some of the bread man yourself.

In Group Worship: Start with fun and games! Your group may choose to have a contest of skills—perhaps a foot race or volleyball tournament. For less athletic groups, try a competitive poetry reading or an exhibition of arts and crafts. Encourage all to try their hand at something. Your friends may surprise you, and you may even surprise yourself. Ask members of the group to offer brief workshops introducing their own special arts and skills.

This is also a time for making an offering to Lugh of the "first fruits" of the harvest. Many groups use a "corn dolly" (made of husks wrapped around a corncob, and decorated with cornsilk for "hair") to symbolize this. Others offer herbs and grains to a sacred fire. Afterward, enjoy a festive time together, doing things that bind you together with happy memories. Dancing, singing, cooking, and feasting are traditional, but this being August, perhaps swimming would be appropriate too!

Suggestion: This is an excellent time of the year to hold or attend a large festival. Organizing such events is a big job that takes lots of people and many practical skills. If it's something that interests you, you may wish to consider volunteering at another festival for a couple of years to learn more about how it works. For your first event, gather a willing group of people to put on a one-day open Pagan gathering, perhaps in a public park. Include some of the elements mentioned earlier, such as contests and feasting. Consider holding a "market day," perhaps setting up a table where members of the group can offer their crafts, used books, or excess ritual gear for sale or trade.

If you are part of a regular group, consider a ritual that raises energy to strengthen your ties to one another, so that you may all work together in harmony.

Fall Equinox (September 21)

History: After the harvest was in, the work wasn't done, for the fields had to be manured and then plowed again, allowing the frost to penetrate the soil and keep it fertile. Grain had to be flailed and stored, sometimes in large pits that may have later been used for ritual purposes. We have no evidence for an equinox festival in Celtic tribes, quite possibly because there was too much to do!

Many Wiccans refer to this festival as Mabon, after a "young god" archetype found in Welsh mythology. There's no real evidence that this was a widely worshiped deity in pre-Christian times, and his name appears to mean "son," which might be applied to any number of gods. While the Mabon archetype is a common one in European mythology and a valid ritual inspiration, my own inclination is to invoke the hammer-god Sucellos, who can be linked through art and artifacts to the protection of the harvest.

In Solitary Worship: If you have a garden, you may be spending time in it, bringing in the things that have grown and eating or preserving them, then preparing the ground for winter. If you don't have a garden, think about planning an enjoyable harvest-time experience, such as apple picking.

For a harvest altar, use gourds, corn husks, autumn leaves, and other seasonal items. Fill a bowl or wicker cornucopia with symbols of the things you have been working on all year, the successes and lessons you bring with you into the dark time ahead. For your Fall Equinox ritual, make a crown of fall leaves by twisting flower wire around the stems, then twisting the pieces together into a circle, or by decorating a small twig or straw wreath with colored leaves. You can make a necklace of acorns obtained from nature, using jewelry wire to fasten them to a chain or cord, or string predrilled acorns obtained from a craft or bead store.

As you did at the Spring Equinox, take time to consider the question of balance in your life. If you find more balance is needed, make a personal commitment to one action that will bring things more into alignment.

It is no coincidence that the school year starts in September, for schools in earlier centuries had to organize their schedule around the times when children were needed to bring in crops. Even in highly industrialized nations, public schools in some areas still shut down at harvest time. While the association of September with learning is obviously a modern one, the quest for knowledge is entirely in keeping with what we know of the Celtic mind. If you're in school, intentionally commit yourself to gaining wisdom, perfecting your skills, and working toward your goals. If you're not in school, find something new to learn. Choose one "serious" book—

perhaps one on Celtic history—and encourage yourself to finish it by Samhain.

Suggestion: In the spirit of Sucellos' hammer, design a ritual that includes grinding grain or herbs (perhaps with a mortar and pestle) as a symbol of the nurturance of the earth and the work of refining one's own heart, mind, and spirit. Invoke Sucellos and his partner Nantosuelta for fertility blessings, protection of one's own boundaries (physical or otherwise), and healing. Use an actual hammer, a mallet, or a small wooden toy hammer as his symbol, and honor his association with vineyards by making an offering of wine or grape juice.

In Group Worship: Just as the first fruits of the harvest have been the subject of celebration, so there are some traditions around the last ear of corn or stalk of grain to be harvested. None of these can be reliably traced to pre-Christian times, but as Alexei Kondratiev points out in *Celtic Rituals*, they may reflect folk superstitions about the spirits of the land. If you live in an area where harvest time is coming to a close in September, consider setting aside a "last" ear of corn or stalk of wheat for the group to offer to the spirits of your locality.

Consider holding your ritual at sunset, especially if the leaves are in full color at this time. Choose an agricultural deity or divine couple, and find some way to bring the bright blaze of this season into your space. Acknowledge the things you have learned from the natural world, and give thanks for whatever prosperity you enjoy, even if it's just a roof over your head or a few dollars in your pocket. Raise energy to sustain all of you through the winter ahead—materially, physically, and emotionally.

Suggestion: Invoke Sucellos and Nantosuelta in a ritual celebrating lessons learned. Have each participant make a thanks offering of incense or wine (use homemade wine, if any of you makes it) while stating aloud a lesson he or she has learned since the last equinox. Then have each participant take an acorn from a bowl and state a way in which he or she will put that lesson into action in the months ahead.

Samhain (October 31)

History: Early medieval Irish texts discuss a celebration held late in the fall, when soldiers and traders came back from afar and livestock was gathered into winter quarters. In these Irish tales, Samhain was a time for tribal assemblies and councils, which are mostly recorded as occasions for feasting, brawling, and boasting. The Saxon historian and monk Bede records this as a time when excess livestock were slaughtered as sacrifices (and, presumably, feast food) to avoid the cost of feeding them through the winter. Though the evidence is fragmentary, most Wiccans now accept that Samhain was the end and beginning of the Celtic year.

We have no direct evidence that the Celts were particularly connected to the spirit world or to the dead at this time, but centuries of belief and decades of recent ritual have confirmed these as standard elements of the Samhain ritual. Bonfires are common at this time, as well as customs adapted from Christian rituals, such as ringing bells for the dead and offering cakes and drinks for the souls of the departed.

Because of the modern customs of Halloween, when parents and homeowners often have responsibilities and many people are holding purely non-religious celebrations, some Wiccans choose to celebrate Samhain on a day other than October 31. Others stick with that date, but move their rituals later into the evening so as not to be interrupted by trick-or-treaters. If you're planning an outdoor rite on Samhain night, it might be wise to let your neighbors and the local police know what you plan to do, so you're not mistaken for Halloween hooligans.

If you practice a form of divination such as Tarot or runes, this is a good time to perform a reading. While there are many divination systems that advertise themselves as "Celtic," perhaps the ones that come closest to anything used in ancient times are the ones that rely on the *ogham* (pronounced "ohm") system of writing, which flourished in Ireland in the fourth through sixth centuries. Ogham inscriptions—based on a limited alphabet and incised as a pattern of straight lines—can be found on the edges of stones, and one of the Roman writers tells of seeing strange sticks carved with writing. These may have been used for divination. The surviving stone inscriptions are largely memorials to the dead, which further links *ogham* to this holiday.

This form of writing is probably linked to Ogma, an Irish god of eloquence and poetry, and Ogmios, a Gaulish god depicted as a bald old man who gathered others about him through charming speech (shown as chains leading from his followers' ears to the god's mouth). There are several systems of using *ogham* characters for divination. It's important to remember that we have no evidence the Celts used *ogham* in this way. You can use a system that makes sense to you, or make up your own. The easiest way to do this is to carve the characters on small sticks of wood, then store them in a small cloth or leather pouch. Bring out the sticks at Samhain. If working with a small group, have each person draw a single stick. For yourself, draw three and throw them at random onto the ground or a table, then read them from bottom to top, as indicating something about your past, present, and future.

Most systems of "Celtic" divination ascribe different trees to each *ogham* letter. Some letters may have been named after trees, but we don't have a clear, historically based idea of what deeper meaning those names carried, or whether the names had any deeper significance at all. Much of what is believed about Celtic tree alphabets and their mystical meaning comes from Robert Graves, a poet and author who wrote about the trees' significance in his book *The White Goddess*. This book has been accepted by many as historical truth; rather, it is a poetic interpretation of facts the author didn't fully understand and molded to match his own theories. As a poetic work, it still carries some value, but it would be a mistake to read it as history.

Several systems exist in which a modern author has used the Celtic tree names for the letters and come up with divinatory meanings for each tree, in some cases based on Celtic lore. The system I use focuses not on trees but on the gift of written language, and was devised simply by choosing an old Irish word for each *ogham* letter and drawing a meaning from that word.

B—*bran* (raven).
You are being summoned for a great event, and will be tested. Your best work and energy are needed now.

L—*lebor* (book).
Others have trod this path before. Learn from their experience before moving forward.

F—*folcaim* (wash, bathe).
Purify yourself physically, spiritually, and emotionally before proceeding.

S—*serc* (love).
Act out of the highest motives and for the good of all. An omen of good fortune.

N—*nephni* (nothing).
Your efforts will be fruitless. Alternately, a blank slate on which you can work your will.

H—*huarn* (cave).
Protect that which is most important to you, perhaps by withdrawing it from public view.

D—*delb* (to form or shape something).
Your outcome depends on the quality of your craftsmanship. Be artful in shaping your life.

T—*tet* (fire).
The forces at work are powerful and can bring either comfort or harm. Shed light by telling your truth.

⦀ C—*cend* (head).
Your own soul or another's may be at stake. Use your mental and spiritual energies to learn more.

⦀ Q—*quert* (apple).
A rare and sweet gift, either about to come or already yours.

M—*melim* (grind).
Purify yourself physically, spiritually, and emotionally before proceeding.

G—*geas* (spell or taboo).
Keep your promises, no mater how difficult it may be. A reminder to use magic wisely.

Ng—*ngetal* (reed).
It is necessary to compromise to preserve what you value.

St—*stán* (tin).
The raw materials are at your disposal. Use them toward a goal both practical and beautiful.

R—*rind* (star).
Look beyond the ordinary world and dare to dream of great journeys and heroic deeds.

A—*abann* (river).
Flow with the situation. All things are washed away in time.

O—*ordd* (hammer).
You have the power to change things (and yourself) drastically. Use this power if it is right to do so.

U—*úaine* (time, opportunity).
Make your move. The people, resources, and energy you need will be there.

|||| E—*erbaim* (trust, bequeath).
Indicates a need to create something that will last beyond your lifetime.

||||| I—*inis* (island).
Your resources are within you. You have the power of self-preservation. Spend time alone in meditation.

In Solitary Worship: Among Wiccans, Samhain is recognized as a time when "the veil is thin" between this world and the realms of the spirit. Many people use this time for divination or communicating with the dead.

Even if you're attending a group event for Samhain, this is a good time to take some time for yourself. Decorate an altar with symbols of people (and animals) who have died, and who are somehow meaningful to you. Set out some food and drink for them, and light a candle or lamp in their honor. This can be a quick remembrance before you head to a gathering, or a more elaborate ritual commemoration.

If you are at a crossroads or plateau in your life, consider using this time to ask the gods and goddesses of your worship to guide you. If you have been planning to form a connection with a particular deity, start a new meditation system or create some manifestation of your religion in the "real" world, now is a good time to start. Many people even get married at Samhain. This may be particularly appropriate if some of the people you love best have died, for popular Wiccan belief holds that this is an easy time for them to be present and witness our acts.

If you are a hunter or warrior in real life, this may be a time to acknowledge the life force you have taken and will take. Give thanks for the benefits you have received from this taking, while asking the gods for continued skill and good fortune.

Suggestion: Devote your Samhain ritual to Cernunnos, who presides over the cycles of life and death and the mysteries of the dark forest. If you can do so safely, walk at night in a wooded place, and use your walking as a form of meditation, with a small part of your mind focusing on keeping you upright and moving while the rest of you contemplates the beauty of the woods. If it is better not to be outdoors on this night, then bring some woodland items in, and use a candle or lamp as a symbolic bonfire. Make an offering of food and drink to the god, and ask that he stand by you in the year ahead, protecting you from harm and guiding your hands to strike out toward your goals. At the end of the rite, choose one of your *ogham* sticks as an indicator of what awaits you in the year ahead.

In Group Worship: This is one gathering that really ought to be held at night. Commemorate the ones you love who have died, perhaps by having each person place a picture or symbolic object on the altar and say a few words about his or her loved one. Write messages to your loved ones on small pieces of parchment and cast them into a bonfire, fireplace or well-shielded cauldron, with the intent that the smoke will carry your messages to the next world. Many groups hold a "dumb supper" in honor of the dead, remaining silent through the entire meal and setting one or more empty places for those who have died.

One group I know has a Samhain tradition of tolling a bell while reading the names of those who were killed in the witchcraft scare at Salem, Massachusetts, in 1692. These victims weren't Wiccans, of course, but were killed through intolerance and hatred. Their names are included in the ritual as symbols of the fight against such senseless tragedy. If your group is involved in religious freedom, environmentalism, or some other cause, you may wish to use this time to renew your commitment to it and perhaps to honor some past heroes and heroines of that cause.

Finally, perform some form of divination. Usually this relies on some outer form such as the *ogham* sticks, Tarot, or a crystal ball, but it can simply take the form of listening to the wind or watching the sky, and communicating the messages received.

Suggestion: Collect dry autumn leaves and let each participant select one. Light a bonfire, either in a fireproof cauldron or outdoors in a safe place. In your ritual, invoke Cernunnos and ask him to help you as you cast out that which is dead or no longer needed. Choose something in your life that you wish to cast out—fear, anxiety, a bad relationship, even poverty—and put your leaf upon the fire, proclaiming "Cernunnos, hear me: Thus I cast out fear!" (or whatever). The group should repeat the phrase to reinforce each member's intent. Then make individual offerings of incense or grain to the fire, proclaiming, "Cernunnos, strengthen me: This I offer for strength!" or whatever positive qualities you wish to bring into your life in the year ahead. Again, the group should support each member's wish with its energy. Informally, after the ritual and meal, have members demonstrate forms of divination or do readings for one another.

As you travel through the year, make a few notes on what was most and least effective in your celebrations. This will help you focus your time and energy on those traditions that are most worthy of revisiting year after year, and sharing with your family and community. One effective way to honor the Wheel of the Year might be to visit the same natural place for each festival, and record what has changed (by writing it down, drawing pictures, or taking photographs).

Sometimes it may not be possible to arrange a ritual for each of the eight festivals. Try at least to spend some time noticing the natural world at such times, and perhaps find a moment to drink a toast to the spirits of the place where you are.

EIGHT

Ethics

Today's world is vastly different from the one the Celtic people knew. In a Celtic community, most people grew up knowing the same rules. For instance, if someone came to your home, you offered hospitality first and asked his or her business later. Celtic religion did not specify an ethical system because everyone already knew how to behave. With Christianity, and with an increasingly multicultural world, came the first widespread association of ethical systems with faith (though some groups, such as the Jews, had followed ethical-religious rules for centuries).

As a modern religion in a multifaceted world, Wicca has its own set of ethics. The early Wiccans summarized these as (roughly) "if it harm none, do what you will." In this chapter, I'll discuss some of the common ethical issues that come up in connection with this religion, applying Celtic concepts where possible.

Of course, this chapter can't possibly cover everything. Your own gods are a good source of guidance, but do not neglect your inner voice and the voices of wise people around you. "Harm none" is a good general guide, a target to aspire to and a reference point when making decisions. Remember that harming yourself is as much an ethical violation as harming another.

Along with "harm none" comes a Wiccan precept often called the Threefold Law. It's a modern expression of an age-old idea. According to this "law," any energy you put forth comes back to you three times. Do a healing spell, and healing will come to you three times in the future. Act unethically toward another, and three times you will be a victim of others' unethical behavior. Not all Wiccans believe in this law, and some of those who do believe it applies only to magical acts. Whether or not you take it literally, it is a useful test. Our actions in this world do have effects beyond the ones we can see or sense. The more you become attuned to divine and magical energies, the more thoughtful you are likely to become in assessing the possible consequences of your acts.

These two concepts combined are a powerful statement of personal responsibility. You can learn any set of guidelines (including the ones that follow), and you can also break them any time you choose. All you have to do is deal with the consequences.

Another way of explaining this is: Wiccan ethics are motivated in part by the idea of personal sovereignty. You may not be chieftain of the tribe, or the best warrior or healer, but you own yourself. You are responsible for managing your resources, and deciding how much you can afford to give to any situation. You are responsible for deciding what your goals are, and taking actions to achieve them. You are responsible for acting toward others in ways that do honor to yourself and the gods of your worship.

Spellwork

We know that the Druids practiced forms of magic for healing, legal victories, and war. We don't know whether they had any particular ethical system for such magical workings. Wiccans today believe in the right of all people to pursue their own fates without magical interference. For this reason, it is considered unwise to do any form of spellwork, even the most benign, for another person without his or her permission.

One area where this often comes up for beginners is "love spells." Many newcomers to Wicca think there's some magical witchy word or working that will get them the love or sex they want. Of course there's no such thing. If you want to find love, you need to appear clean and well-groomed, do things that are interesting to you so you'll have something to talk about, go places where you'll meet suitable people, be friendly and considerate to everyone, and let all your friends know you're single and looking.

No one is worth having if he or she has to be forced. Even if spells could bring you a lover, would that really be worthwhile? The only ethical form of love spell is the one you do for yourself, asking divine help in being the best and most desirable person you can be, and trusting in the gods and goddesses of your faith to bring the opportunity that's right for you. (You also have to do all the things I said in the last paragraph.)

Another ethical question involves "negative" spells. You *can* do a spell to harm someone, and can expect that such a working would be effective. This is where the Threefold Law serves as a guideline. Is it worth it to you to suffer three times the harm you are about to mete out? Usually, the answer is no.

A cautionary tale: Once, two friends were sharing an apartment in a wooded place where they loved the trees and the privacy. Their landlord decided the place would be more attractive to tenants if it had a lawn, so he brought in machines to tear out the trees. The two friends were outraged. They knew they would get in trouble if they physically harmed the equipment, so instead they did a magical working to make the machines break. It worked. The machines broke down, and the project was significantly delayed. But in the meantime, the Threefold Law kicked in: Both friends' cars and their toilet malfunctioned. They risked losing their jobs because they couldn't make it to work, and let's just say their sanitary arrangements were rather primitive for a few days. Eventually, the landlord brought in new machines and tore out the trees anyway.

What would be another way to go about this? Many Wiccans do protective spells for their homes and possessions. Instead of seeking to destroy others' property, the friends might have put a spell on the trees to protect them from harm. A common way to handle negativity is to use a mirror spell, in which a mirror is empowered to reflect back all negativity aimed at it. This isn't actively doing harm to anyone—unless *they* set out to do harm. A tree protection spell might have involved burying small mirrors in the ground, facing outward, at each side of the stand of trees.

Or, on a more prosaic level, the two friends might have accepted the fact that the landlord owned the trees and could do as he liked with them, and instead put their energy toward finding a more tree-friendly place to live.

Here's another warning: When designing rituals, avoid placing one participant in the role of sacrificial "victim" or having someone pretend to die during a ritual. (For instance, some Wiccans believe that the harvest god dies at Lugnasadh, and write rituals where a participant enacts this by walking up to a fire or lying on the ground.) This role is a part of many ancient tales and folk customs, and designing a ritual around such customs may seem harmless, for of course you wouldn't let any actual injury be done to someone. Still, I know of a couple of examples in which someone took on such a role and suffered a personal tragedy in the weeks following the ritual. Coincidence? Perhaps. Yet if you use this theme—a perfectly valid one with ancient roots—it may be best to offer an object, rather than a person, to symbolize the victim.

Healing

When done ethically, healing rituals can be very effective, and there are historical examples of healing rites, such as the Druids' cutting of mistletoe and the small metal or bone body parts found as sacrifices to the gods. These may provide ideas in designing a healing rite for yourself or another.

It is always OK to do healing work on yourself. The issues come up when the ill person is someone else. It can be heart-wrenching: Someone you care about is suffering, and you feel helpless. The only thing you can think of that will help is a healing spell. Yet you need to make this decision with your mind, not your heart. Do you know that healing is what the person wants? An elderly or very ill person may fear death, or may welcome it. Do you have permission from the ill person to work magic on his or her behalf? It is always better to ask. If you do not have permission but feel compelled to do something magical, you might direct your energies toward "the best possible outcome" for that person, leaving the precise nature of that outcome in the hands of the gods. Other options include working with the person's family to give them strength and peace, or doing a ritual for yourself, asking divine assistance in dealing with the strong feelings that serious health problems can bring out.

Under no circumstances can magic or spellwork take the place of getting the best possible medical care for health problems, and learning as much as you can about your body so that you can take responsibility for your health care decisions.

Sexuality

Wiccans believe that sexuality is sacred, and the scanty Celtic history points to an acceptance and understanding of sexuality, coupled with a social code that seems to have allowed women greater freedom than they had in Greek or Roman societies. Today, it is vital to act ethically in this area of life, for that which is sacred must be handled with *more* care than ordinary.

"All acts of love and pleasure are my rituals," reads the "Charge of the Goddess," a poem that has been through many revisions, but remains the closest thing Wiccans have to a sacred text. In Wiccan communities, homosexual, bisexual, and transgendered people, as well as people in "open" or otherwise unconventional relationships, are likely to find acceptance. Modern Wicca also generally respects the idea that men and women are equal, that neither sex is better or more capable or more spiritual. Many Wiccan books specifically honor goddesses and women's spiritual development, but we now see analogous resources becoming available to men. Wiccans believe biology does not give either sex any rights over the other.

This respect for sexuality is in no way applicable to children and teenagers, or those incapable of giving consent. These are protected by honor as well as law from sexual advances by adults, and from witnessing the sexual activity of adults. Adults who make such advances are regarded as abusers and in many cases banned from Wiccan events.

The principle of personal sovereignty gives you full control over *your* sexuality, which always includes the right to say "no" to any act or relationship. While many adult Wiccans enjoy exploring various forms of sexual expression, it is always appropriate to check with your partners, to respect their boundaries, and to speak up in defense of your own.

These decisions are particularly important for young people, who sometimes don't yet have the life experience to make good decisions in response to pressure. It may be helpful to remember the principles of honor. Avoid any action that requires you to lie, even to yourself. Contain your urges when expressing them would hurt you or another. Stand up for your right to decide what is and isn't good for you. Others may not like your choices, but you are responsible for yours and they are responsible for theirs. Assure yourself and your partners of protection from disease or unwanted pregnancy, and refrain from acts that pose those risks when protection is not available. Honor demands that you act with respect toward the people around you, for by doing otherwise you dishonor yourself, your community, and your gods.

As part of the belief that our bodies are our own, some Wiccan groups or individuals prefer practicing in the nude ("skyclad"). This has an echo in Celtic history, for the Celts' elite warriors were famed for fighting in the nude, possibly for religious reasons. In any case, ritual nudity is a spiritual practice, and should not be understood as an advertisement of sexual availability. It is not ethical to require anyone to disrobe, or to put anyone down for not doing so.

The earliest Wiccans' initiations were sexual in nature, and this

"Great Rite" continues in a few groups. The vast majority of Wiccan groups now perform this in a symbolic way (often using a chalice and ritual knife). It is possible to spend many years as a Wiccan and never attend a ritual where a sexual act is performed. In those groups where it does occur, it is most often done by experienced practitioners who are committed partners, and who may do the actual deed in an area screened off from the other participants. It should *never* be a requirement that you have sex with someone to join a group, learn "mysteries," or undergo initiation. Indeed, sex between a Wiccan teacher and student is frowned on, even when both parties are consenting adults.

Before you think I'm taking all the fun out of everything, let me mention that sex magic is a recognized way of raising energy, and often one that brings great meaning and joy for the participants. This is most effective when the participants are experienced practitioners who are involved in a longstanding, loving partnership, familiar with one another's bodies and rhythms, and in full agreement on what they will do and why they will do it. In such a situation, it is possible to control the moment of physical climax and use its energy toward a magical goal. Properly done, such a working can be very powerful indeed.

Mind-Altering Substances

There are many indications that the ancient Celts enjoyed wine and other alcoholic beverages, and the Druids may have included mind-altering herbs among their healing tools. Today the modern practitioner is faced with a variety of available substances that are said to help the user explore alternate realities.

As always, you have the right to choose to use these, provided you're willing to accept the consequences. The use of such drugs in current Western culture carries costs—economic, legal, and health-related. Most groups have rules against drug use during rituals, and using illegal drugs at a Pagan festival or other large gathering has the potential to bring harm not only to you but to the organizers of the event and the Pagan community in general. More important, as magical aids, mind-altering substances are simply not as effective as the trained and informed mind, a tool that is available to you without altering your body chemistry.

(By the way, this does not apply to medicines or regimens prescribed by a responsible health professional. I've heard of cases where people did serious damage to their health by abandoning their prescriptions in the name of "ritual purity." There are any number of ways to achieve such purity—giving up a bad habit, for example—and it's never necessary to defy medical wisdom in the name of your religion.)

Many Wiccans use wine or other alcoholic beverages (mead, or honey wine, is a favorite) as offerings to the gods and goddesses of their faith, and it is reasonable to suspect that the ancient Celts did the same. As with meat offerings, the god or goddess may have received only a small portion, with the rest being consumed by the participants. However, it is inappropriate to offer alcoholic beverages as the ritual drink in open circles (where underage persons or those with alcohol sensitivities may be present), without offering a non-alcoholic alternative.

My own choice is to use fruit juice unless I am certain wine will be acceptable to all present. If you are offered alcohol in a ritual cup, it is never required that you drink it. Simply lift the cup toward you respectfully without taking any.

Violence and Revenge

The Roman accounts paint the Celts as swift to anger and seek violent revenge. Such behavior seemed barbaric to the Romans, who were more inclined to deal with insults by filing ruinous lawsuits. Vengeful behavior may have made sense among Celtic warriors, whose status system was based on personal valor and support for one's allies. In today's world, such behavior is more likely to get you locked up, and a different approach is required.

The "harm none" rule generally does not prohibit actions taken to preserve the immediate safety of yourself or your family. Beyond that, Wiccans generally believe the gods take care of providing appropriate consequences for those who violate others. Of course ordinary remedies should apply, such as taking a thief to court or breaking up with a partner who lies. But vengeful magical or physical action—even when words are your only weapon—is likely to bring its own consequences upon the one who performs it, in accordance with the Threefold Law.

Even in early medieval Irish laws, a woman could divorce her husband for some kinds of physical abuse. Modern Wiccans condemn both women and men who abuse their partners, children, or other household members. At the same time, we sometimes have to fight court cases alleging that simply bringing up a child as a Wiccan is abusive.

The Broom Closet

Within any group of Wiccans or Pagans, you're likely to find some who are "out of the broom closet"—that is, who are open with the outside world about their religion—and others who prefer to keep their faith quiet. Each person's decision on being public is based on his or her own perceptions of risks, rewards, stakes, and personal safety. It is a serious violation of etiquette and honor to make someone's Wiccan affiliation known without his or her permission.

Likewise, the use of magical names should be respected at Wiccan events, for we each are entitled to make our own decisions about how much of our identities to reveal. If close friends prefer to use their magical names at open events, make an effort not to call them by their real names. When in doubt, it is always better to ask what people want to be called than to guess. It is also unethical to tell people outside your group or community about the places where Wiccans meet, and thus expose them to interference or disruption.

Many other questions on how to behave in Wiccan communities can be solved by good manners. As a host, one should welcome guests and offer them refreshment. As a guest, one should respond to invitations on time, show up when promised, and leave on time. When disagreements occur—whether the topic is the existence of the gods or how to deal with garden slugs—express your point of view politely, offering respect for the other person even as you disagree with his or her ideas. When you are sad or angry about someone's words or actions, take it up with that person in private first, rather than bad-mouthing him or her to the rest of your community.

Finally, whether or not you are public about your religion, it is important to treat other people's faiths with the same respect you seek for your own. You do your religion no favors when you bash others' choices or ethics. The best thing you can do for Wicca is to set an example of tolerance, patience, and a sincere respect for those who are different from you.

Students and Teachers

It is common, but not required, for people just discovering Wicca to spend some time studying with a more experienced person. Enter into these relationships with care. A teacher and student ideally spend a good bit of time together over the course of several months, and their work touches on sensitive areas such as spirituality, values, and emotions. While the Wiccan teaching process is a far cry from the twenty-year Druid training, it can still be a long and intense process, one that requires time, energy, and patience from both teacher and student.

Some teachers offer classes, and learning in a group often leads to the "graduates" forming a Wiccan group together. Others prefer a one-on-one or "apprenticeship" model. It is up to the student to ask for teaching. Expect to be checked out carefully before the teacher agrees, and use the time to make sure this teacher is someone from whom you wish to learn. As a more experienced Wiccan, you'll receive requests for teaching, and will need to evaluate not only whether the student is a good fit with your knowledge and style, but also whether you have sufficient energy, stability, and time at this point in your life for teaching others.

The teacher-student relationship is by its very nature an imbalanced one, and has a logical end at which the student is "initiated." It is never appropriate to engage in romantic or sexual behavior with a Wiccan teacher or student while that relationship is in place, and even after initiation such feelings may pose extra challenges to the people involved. If you find yourself developing romantic or sexual attraction to a teacher or student, you must choose whether to set those feelings aside or find another teacher to finish the training. This can be very disruptive to all involved, and it is the teacher's responsibility to put the student's spiritual development first. It's better to start off knowing that such a relationship simply isn't an option.

It is usually considered unethical to charge money for initiation or admission to a Wiccan group. Many Wiccan courses do cost money, which properly covers the cost of materials or copying. Wiccans usually see no problem with charging money for such skills as Tarot reading or counseling. An ongoing ritual group may ask members to contribute magical supplies or money to buy them. Upon initiation, it is appropriate to offer the teacher some sort of gift, in keeping with your resources.

Groups

There are a number of good books available for people forming or leading Wiccan groups. Wiccan groups are not like churches—they tend to be small groups that meet in outdoor spots or private homes, and their membership often changes from year to year. It's not a sign of failure to be part of a group that dissolves; this happens all the time. A few, however, usually centered around a charismatic individual, have lasted for decades.

Groups sometimes declare certain rituals or parts of rituals to be "secret" or "closed." This practice is common to ceremonial lodges such as the Freemasons. Properly done, such secrecy has the effect of binding the members closer together while focusing the "group mind" on common goals. Once this effect is in operation, it doesn't matter if someone spills the secret! The "secrets" of Masonic practice have been published for decades, yet ethical members of those groups still keep them and find value in them.

Because people in a regular group often use ritual time to work out personal issues, you may come to know things about fellow group members that should be treated as private. Respect their confidences and, where appropriate, offer your support.

One exception: Magical secrets and group confidentiality should never be used to conceal criminal acts or abuse. From time to time, someone misunderstands what Wicca is about or misappropriates its name to pose as an all-knowing leader who demands time, money, control, or sexual favors in exchange for the "mysteries." There is a big difference between this and a healthy student-teacher relationship. If you feel someone is trying to control you, leave the situation as quickly as you can. Wiccans respect the freedom of every individual, and among ethical Wiccans your decisions about your own spiritual life will be respected.

History

Here I'd like to address a subject that is just beginning to become important in Wicca: the ethical treatment of historical material. As a spiritual path, Wicca is a creation of the twentieth century. It is entirely possible to be a Wiccan without any reference to history at all, to celebrate earth and sky, goddess and god, healing and art as a living faith in the here and now. Yet for many of us, history is a vital part of religion, providing inspiration, mystery, and foundation for our acts of worship and creativity.

The earliest Wiccans, living in Great Britain, looked to their homeland's past as a major source of ideas and language. Unfortunately, in their quest to gain legitimacy for the new path, they crafted a body of literature that painted Wicca as a survival from ancient times, a secret supposedly handed down for centuries. Only recently, they claimed, was it possible to reveal this mystery. Along with cloaking themselves in this historical mantle, they drew upon "historical" ideas based in poor scholarship, misinterpretation, and even pure fiction.

Later Wiccans followed this regrettable lead with such distortions as the idea of the "Burning Times," a reference to historical European witch hunts. According to some Wiccan books, nine million women who practiced the Old Religion were burned at the stake. In fact, the people targeted by this form of popular hysteria were much fewer in number, included both women and men, and despite extensive record-keeping cannot be said to have followed any spiritual system resembling Wicca.

Another common myth among Wiccans is that of the Great Goddess, which includes the ideas that at one time everyone worshiped a goddess as a primary deity, that all these goddesses were pretty much the same and that ancient societies were ruled by women. Ancient people certainly worshiped goddesses, but they worshiped gods, too, and the evidence doesn't point to any goddess archetype as being dominant across a wide area. In the Celtic world alone, there are many distinct goddess (and god) types, with different names, attributes, appearances, and sacred places, and little or no evidence of matriarchy. The Great Goddess myth may have been valuable in raising awareness of the religious life of ancient women. But it should not be regarded as historical truth.

The idea of "the Goddess" and "the God," universal male and female energies, is a modern one. It's convenient for Wiccans and Pagans trying to design rituals for large groups. Still, my own preference is to design rituals honoring a historical god, goddess, divine pair, or triple group.

The ancient people whose worship inspires us, and the gods of their worship, deserve respect for their real existence. We can never know what they thought or how they felt or what they believed. To the extent that we can know the facts, it is an act of honor to respect those facts. You can declare almost any idea to be part of your Wiccan worship, and you have every right to do so as a matter of religious faith. But when you start declaring ideas to be historical truth, it's important to rely on facts as far as possible, and on the best available scholarly opinions.

That doesn't mean you have to try to exactly duplicate ancient rituals or beliefs. You live in today's world, however much history may appeal to you, and you were shaped by the culture in which you were raised. It's only natural that your faith and your spirit will to a certain extent be a product of your time and culture. Wicca is living proof that it is OK to create a new religion. What is not OK is to call it history.

In practice, this means being clear, with yourself and with others who worship with you, about what is and isn't drawn from historical fact.

One challenge for Celtic Wiccans is the fact that historians' opinions change over time. Sometimes new evidence indicates a new direction or discredits an accepted idea. Sometimes one scholar goes back and reexamines the work of another and demonstrates an error or a more reasonable interpretation of evidence. The academic world is as subject to fashions and trends as any other, and sometimes an idea just falls out of favor. Often, worthy researchers disagree among themselves. All of these issues pose significant challenges for ordinary people who love history and want to learn more, but who aren't prepared to drop everything and take up an academic career.

The best approach I can suggest is to read widely, familiarizing yourself with as much of the factual evidence as possible, but also getting to know the chief scholars and writers in your area of interest. That way, when they disagree, you can make choices based on your opinion of an author's work as well as how well he or she defends this particular point.

Another way to expand of your historical knowledge might be to spend time learning a Celtic language. This works best when you can practice with other speakers of that language. It might make an excellent project for a Wiccan group to undertake together, if only to add a few authentic Celtic words to a ritual. I haven't done this, for reasons of time and availability of language partners, but I know others who have found it valuable.

Studying history takes time, and you may be saying "Wait! I can't read all that!" For most of us, Celtic history must remain a hobby, squeezed in between other priorities. Take some time to explore when you can, balancing your learning with the other parts of your life, and don't feel guilty for not being able to do it all. Push yourself to read a scholarly book or article when you can, or even just spend time looking at photos of Celtic art. It may also help to decide on a specialized area that interests you and learn all you can about it. Use what you learn to inform and inspire your worship, and be willing to make changes when you uncover new information or recognize your own mistakes.

Why is all this historical stuff important? Three reasons: Honesty, honor, and learning. Honesty with yourself is an important practice, necessary for growth; honesty with your community shows respect, and earns it in return. Treating history with dignity does honor to the gods and goddesses of your worship, and to those who have traveled this path before you. Finally, the study of history has long been recognized as an excellent way to improve your thinking skills and make it easier for you to learn and grow. This, in the end, is one of the chief goals of spiritual work.

With this thought, we come to the end of this book. If you're about to flip to the Bibliography and start looking for more books to read, more ideas for learning, then I've done my job! My experience of Celtic Wicca is one of learning to become a better person, to understand more of the world around me, and to create beauty and good with the powers available to me. I wish you the same, or something better.

Bibliography

Three Excellent Books

The Pagan Religions of the Ancient British Isles, Ronald F. Hutton (Blackwell, 1993). Outlines what we do know about ancient religion, directly tackling some common pseudo-historic ideas. Takes the Wiccan/Pagan movement seriously while calling for a rigorous approach to facts.

Celtic Rituals: An Authentic Guide to Ancient Celtic Spirituality, Alexei Kondratiev (Collins, 1998, also published under the title *The Apple Branch*). While not specifically Wiccan, Kondratiev's rituals are based in a deep scholarly and spiritual understanding of Celtic history.

Symbol and Image in Celtic Religious Art, Miranda Green (Routledge, 1989). A very useful look at the available evidence of Celtic religions.

Three Good Books About Celtic History

The Celtic World, edited by Miranda Green (Routledge, 1995). A compendium of articles on a wide variety of historical and modern subjects. Particularly useful for its sections on Celtic art and Peter J. Reynolds's article on Celtic farming.

The Ancient World of the Celts, Peter Berresford Ellis (Constable, 1998). Goes beyond the standard categories of history to discuss Celtic physicians, road builders, and craftsmen.

The Ancient Celts, Barry Cunliffe (Oxford, 1997). Well-designed book combining authoritative history with excellent illustrations.

Three Good Books About Celtic Religion

Dictionary of Celtic Mythology, James MacKillop (Oxford, 1998). A handy reference for names and places.

Pagan Celtic Britain, Anne Ross (Academy Chicago, 1996). One of the first compendiums of historical evidence. Despite some dated information

(it was first published in 1967), this book is still useful, especially for its
treatment of animal symbolism.

The Druids, Stuart Piggott (Thames and Hudson, 1968). A look at the evidence for ancient priesthoods and the way that evidence has been (mis)interpreted in recent centuries.

THREE GOOD BOOKS ABOUT WICCA FOR NEWCOMERS AND YOUNG PEOPLE

Wicca for the Solitary Practitioner, Scott Cunningham (Llewellyn, 1990). Many people start with this book. Pleasant and simple spells and ideas for crafting your own.

Spell Craft, Lilith McClelland (Eschaton, 1997). Written specifically for younger audiences, this book is a favorite among teens.

Life Magic: The Power of Positive Witchcraft, Susan Bowes (Simon and Schuster, 1999). Illustrated introduction to many of the systems common to Wiccans.

THREE GOOD BOOKS ABOUT WICCA

The Triumph of the Moon: A History of Modern Pagan Witchcraft, Ronald F. Hutton (Oxford, 2000). Hutton, a historian, traces the roots of the modern Wiccan movement, shattering some myths and providing much food for thought. Focuses on Britain.

Drawing Down the Moon: Witches, Druids, Goddess-Worshipers and Other Pagans in America Today, Margot Adler (Penguin, 1997). An American journalist's view of Wicca and related movements. Somewhat dated despite an update from the 1979 edition, but a useful look at the roots of modern American Pagan worship.

Persuasions of the Witch's Craft, Tanya Luhrmann (Harvard, 1991). Luhrmann, a sociologist, studied modern Wiccans and magicians in Britain.

THREE GOOD BOOKS ABOUT CEREMONIAL MAGIC

Psychic Self-Defense and Well-Being, Dion Fortune (Weiser, 1993, first published 1930). A classic text on the subject, outlining a technique that can be adapted to many circumstances.

Inside a Magical Lodge: Group Ritual in the Western Tradition, John Michael Greer (Llewellyn, 1998). Traces the history of the lodge movement and provides an excellent template for a working magical group.

Dancers to the Gods: The Magical Records of Charles Seymour and Christine Hartley, 1937–1939, Alan Richardson (Aquarian, 1985). A valuable, in-depth look at a long-term magical working involving two experienced practitioners.

THREE GOOD BOOKS ABOUT THE CELTO-ROMAN PERIOD

The Celts and the Classical World, David Rankin (Routledge, 1987). An excellent overview of the historical encounters between the two cultures.

Religion in Roman Britain, Martin Henig (Batsford, 1984). Argues for the pervasive influence of Roman belief in the Celto-Roman period.

Ireland and the Classical World, Philip Freeman (University of Texas, 2001). The Romans never invaded Ireland, but the two cultures did interact. Excellent presentation with original Greek, Latin, and Irish texts for the scholar, with English translations for the general reader.

THREE GOOD BOOKS FOR WICCAN/PAGAN FAMILIES

Pagan Parenting: Spiritual, Magical and Emotional Development of the Child, Kristin Madden (Llewellyn, 2000). Excellent resource including information on community and legal topics, plus unique ideas on helping children understand their own magical abilities.

Celebrating the Great Mother: A Handbook of Earth-Honoring Activities for Parents, Cait Johnson (Inner Traditions, 1995). Good ideas and activities, though rather Goddess-oriented.

Circle Round: Raising Children in Goddess Traditions, Starhawk (Bantam, 1998). Hands-on approach with songs, stories, craft projects, and recipes for family learning and growth.

THREE USEFUL BOOKS

The Master Book of Herbalism, Paul Beyerl (Phoenix, 1984). Offers both magical and medicinal qualities of herbs.

Food and Drink in Britain: From the Stone Age to the 19th Century, C. Anne Wilson (Academy Chicago, 1991). No recipes, but enough information to inspire a period meal, and substantial detail of what was and wasn't eaten in various stages of history.

The Art of the Celts, Lloyd and Jennifer Laing (Thames and Hudson, 1992). Good source of ideas for incorporating authentic Celtic themes into visual art.

Index

Abann (A), 172
Adler, Margot, 111
Agriculture (farming), 152–53, 154–56,
    159–60, 168
Allason-Jones, Lindsay, 75
Altars
    creating your own, 24–25
    tools used, 25–27
Amulets, guardian, 137–39
Animals
    Cernunnos and, 60, 63, 64
    Epona and, 56, 58
Aphrodite, 65
Apollo, 59
Apprenticeships, 185–86
Aquae Sulis, 89–90, 93
Artifacts (art objects), Celtic, 5–6, 88–89
    burial practices and, 9, 124
    creative tradition and, 110–11, 113–14
    magical tools, 25–26
Art, sacrifice of, for rituals, 123–28
Ash trees, 10, 25
Athames (ritual knives), 26, 35
Attire (clothing), 27–28, 113–14

Banisher, the, 142–44
Baths (bathing), 114, 153–54
    Cerridwen ritual, 79–81
Bede, 169
Belenus, 160–62
Bell, Martin, 9
Beltane (May 1), 155–59
Bidding farewell, in rituals, 29
Birds and birdsong, 155
Blessings, 148
    Rosmerta candle, 66–69

Bonfires, 151–52, 157, 174–75
Books, reading for rituals, 87–89
    ethical treatment of historical material,
        187–90
    recommended, 191–93
Boudicca, 12, 137
Bran (B), 171
Bread, 165
Brigantes, 6, 7
Brigid (Brid; St. Bridget; Brigantia), 6, 7,
    13, 44–49, 134–35
    in daily life, 48–49
    at Imbolc, 150–51
    spell, 45–48
Burial (funeral) practices, 7–8, 14, 38, 164

Caeilte, 139
Calendar, 145–46
    Christian, 3n, 153
    of seasonal rituals, 145–75
Calling of the Four Winds, 104–5
Calling the Quarters, 29, 40–42
Candlemas, 150
Candles, 127, 148, 151
    for altars, 25
    gazing at (meditation exercise), 16–17
    Rosmerta blessing with, 66–69
Cars, Epona and, 54, 57–58
Casting a circle, 28, 30–31, 32–34
Celebration rituals, 85–86
Celtic circles, 36–38
Celtic Rituals (Kondratiev), 168
Celts
    burial practices, 7–8, 14, 164
    ideals of, 139–41
    myths about, 4–5, 187–90

195